Pup Culture

PUP CULTURE

STORIES, TIPS, AND THE IMPORTANCE OF ADOPTING A DOG

VICTORIA LILY SHAFFER

TILLER PRESS

New York London Toronto Sydney New Delhi

TILLER PRESS

An Imprint of Simon & Schuster, Inc.
1230 Avenue of the Americas
New York, NY 10020

First Tiller Press hardcover edition October 2021

TILLER PRESS and colophon are registered trademarks of
Simon & Schuster, Inc.

For information about special discounts for bulk purchases,
please contact Simon & Schuster Special Sales at 1-866-506-1949
or business@simonandschuster.com.

The Simon & Schuster Speakers Bureau can bring authors to your
live event. For more information or to book an event, contact the
Simon & Schuster Speakers Bureau at 1-866-248-3049 or visit our
website at www.simonspeakers.com.

Interior design by Matthew Ryan

Manufactured in China

10   9   8   7   6   5   4   3   2   1

Library of Congress Cataloging-in-Publication Data has been applied for.

ISBN 978-1-9821-7882-6
ISBN 978-1-9821-7883-3 (ebook)

Emily and Echo

In loving memory of Emily Callaway,
a supportive friend, rescue advocate,
and my dogs' biggest fan. ♥ I know
she's reading this book among the
most adorable puppies in heaven.

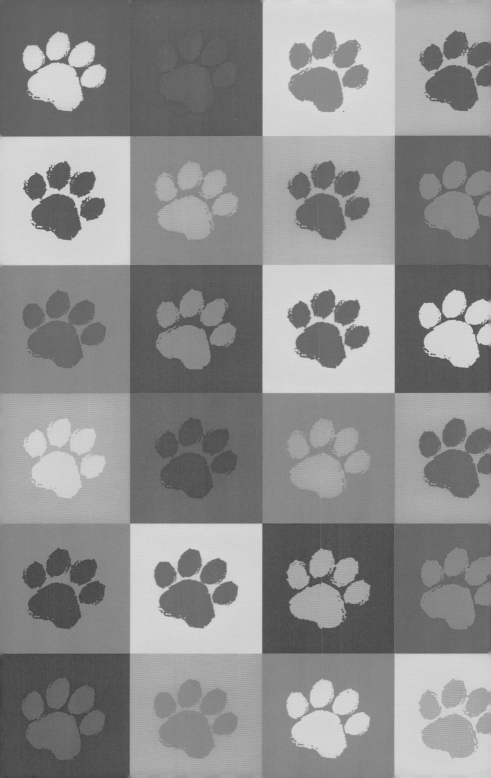

CONTENTS

What have I done to deserve this? Absolutely nothing!

As I read through the pages of my daughter's first book, I'm struck by the pride I feel in the work she does, how good she is at it, and how little I had to do with it. In fact, I appear to have been a force she had to outsmart before proceeding with her mission, and I'm grateful that was relatively easy for her.

Certainly, as a cat man—my childhood cat's name was Cleo—I wasn't about to teach my kids love and caring by getting them a *dog*. When it comes to preaching family love, the cat-man-do works alone! (Forgive me.) Yet something in then ten-year-old Victoria made her lead every family bike ride we took in the city to make a stop at the pet shop, "just to visit the puppies." As she and her brother, Will, climbed joyfully into the pens with the various shih tzus and labradoodles, how could I have known that Victoria was engaging me in subtle "dognitive" therapy (again, your forgiveness)?

It was hard to miss how happy the kids were in the company of dogs. When the biking conversation on the way home centered on puppy-cuteness ratings, I freely participated in a noncommittal way. What I didn't count on—but was consistently confronted with—was Victoria's innate nurturing sensibility. This was an ingrained predi-

lection toward caring and protectiveness, which she showed from an early age. This was evident to me while on a camping trip with my old boss, the outdoorsy David Letterman. Victoria looked at me and instinctively realized that Jews shouldn't camp and that I needed her help. She fed me, removed my shoes, and tucked me into a sleeping bag, transforming me into, yes, a happy camper when I really needed to be one.

Imagine when this level of compassion gets applied to members of a four-legged species who want nothing more than to love and be loved. The results are combustible, and Victoria exploded into a crusader for dog rescue, a selfless rescuer herself and an expert in the emotional and physical care of dogs. This is a win-win, for her and for dogs everywhere.

How did I luck out and end up with a daughter whose internal kindness governs her goodness and who, along with my son, Will, makes me the proudest of dads? Well, it must have been because of Cathy, their mother: I married the right girl.

— *Paul Shaffer*

One

TO THE RESCUE!

— ❧ —

THE DOGS THAT CHANGED MY LIFE

My parents didn't grow up with dogs, and they weren't dog lovers.

If we ever went to someone's house and they had dogs, my mom would force a half smile and brush them off her lap. My dad would chuckle through a "Whoa!" with the same uncomfortable hesitation he had when our family went paragliding in Wyoming. And before you accuse me of overexaggerating—I know no dog could be as frightening as looking down at your shoes dangling so many feet above the ground, but what can I say? My dad has is-shoes (he's cursed me with the need to make bad puns—sorry).

Every summer, my family drove to East Hampton to visit the Makrianes-Gravels. Their daughter Maysie became one of my best friends (she'll also reappear later in this book). We had a yearly routine—Maysie would always force me to dive into the freezing ocean with her like we were participating in a polar bear plunge. The boys, my little brother William (Will for short) and her little brother Jimmy, would play video games all day. Our parents would spend evenings chatting and drinking wine, and Lia—the Makrianes-Gravels' middle child—as we always joked, "hung out with the dogs." She already knew what I'd yet to learn: dogs over humans, always and anytime.

It was during these summers with the Makrianes-Gravel family that I first started to truly enjoy and connect with dogs. During beach BBQs, their dogs would be the life of the party. They'd run in circles, dive into the frigid ocean to fetch balls, and roll happily in the sand. You best believe those beach traditions came full circle when I drove the first dogs of my adult life, Rue and Echo, to the beach in East Hampton within days of adopting them.

Rue's first trip to the beach.

Maysie's dogs left an impression. I can name every dog she had since we were two years old better than I can name the presidents of the United States. I have vivid memories of us walking Spike and Molly, and I could never forget Pippa, the blind shih tzu with no teeth. Maysie's mom, Anne, had taken Pippa from their neighbors once she discovered they wanted to put him down preemptively. He was the first ill dog I'd ever seen. I remember thinking it was so cool that Anne had stepped in to save Pippa, even if he was disheveled and scary to look at. As I watched Anne lovingly administer all Pippa's different medications to him one summer afternoon in the kitchen, I realized, *That's going to be me one day.* As a side note, this past Christmas, Anne took in a senior Chihuahua named Jude who I struggled to get adopted. He had a handful of health issues

Spike & Molly

and snapped without warning. Jude is now doing better than ever! Anne really can't say no to any dog, and she's amazing for that.

The shift in my brother and me was immediate. Back home in Bedford, New York, Will and I constantly begged our parents for a dog. We dreamed about what breed we would get and what names we would choose. A couple of times my parents tried to grant our wish, spending way too much money on "designer dogs" from award-winning breeders that friends had recommended (ah, the privilege that money affords). My mom's friend swore a bichon frise like hers would be the perfect dog for our family because "they don't shed," but Tyler, our tiny bichon puppy, was much too yappy for my mom's liking.

Tyler, the bichon

A year later, another friend guilted my parents into thinking they'd chosen the wrong breed. "Never get a small dog. They're harder to train and never shut up," they said. "Get a golden retriever. They're the best." But Candy, our golden retriever puppy, was seriously out to get Will. I have vivid memories of being stranded on our backyard playground set because Candy was aggressively barking down below, on a mission to bite my brother's tiny limbs. (My future self has learned that any breed of dog can be aggressive without proper training and exercise. Are you surprised that the ever-so-popular husky and Chihuahua are on the aggressive breeds list?)

This is all to say that neither puppy lasted more than a week in the Shaffer household, and they were summarily returned to their breeders' care. Somehow these breed-related hiccups (or in Will's case, major trauma) didn't deter us from desperately wanting and asking for another puppy each year. We knew if we asked enough times that my parents—the type who always did their best to give us everything to not deprive us of "normal childhood experiences"— would cave for another four-legged family member neither of them wanted.

I was hopeful the next puppy we brought into our home would be "the one." However, it wasn't until the age of twelve, after looking at tons of websites selling pocket beagles ("But *Mommm*, this dog will fit in your pocket!") and teacup Yorkies (seriously, how are they made so tiny?!), that I stumbled upon two amazing websites: petfinder.com and adoptapet.com. These sites are hubs to find pets available for adoption, and the listings just go on and on. The photos posted on these sites were unlike others I'd seen on breeders' sites. There were no designer pooches sleeping on clouds or puppies tucked into baskets filled with rose petals. These dogs often arrive at the rescues and shelters looking helpless, malnourished, and filthy, many of them pictured inside kennels with their little noses pushed through chain-link fences, desperate for human attention. After spending hours scrolling through listings and clicking for pictures and details, I wanted to save them all. Many late nights were spent researching on my flower-power Macintosh computer (who remembers those?) until my parents would bust me at 3 a.m., ordering me to finally go to sleep.

Rescue and adoption weren't trendy topics in the early 2000s. After simple Google searches introduced me to the horrors of animal abuse and puppy mills, I prepared educational speeches for the rides to school that resembled a bad car commercial:

> Did you know adoption saves lives, Mom? It's true! Every time someone adopts a dog, there's room to take in another. Forget paying breeders thousands of dollars: you can get a one-of-a-kind mutt for the mere price of an adoption fee. Not only are rescue dogs more unique but they also get all the best qualities from the breeds they're mixed with. Did I mention they're healthier, too? Genetically they're much stronger!

It's become a joke among friends and family that I preach to everyone, multiple times, about my latest and most loved product discoveries. For example, most recently, I touted the Trader Joe's hair serum ("It's only $3.99 and will defrizz your hair and make it as soft as a puppy's belly—you gotta get it!") and the Italian Volcano organic lemon juice from Costco ("It's one hundred percent organic, and when added to a glass of water, it makes hydrating a breeze. Think lemonade without the sugar!"). As you can tell, I gushed the same way about these sites, and about dog adoption and rescue in general. It was enough to drive my parents crazy. But what can I say? I become very passionate about all sorts of things—from animal rescue to delicious lemon juice—and I want to share my discoveries with everyone.

My convincing and "selling" didn't stop there. I sent and forwarded emails, too (something I get from my mother). After hundreds of messages containing links to adoptable puppies alongside false promises (i.e., *I'll do the laundry*; *I'll never fight with you again*; *I'll go to sleep on time*; *I'll eat whatever you serve for dinner no matter how dry it is*), my mom finally cracked when a litter of black puppies with long floppy ears was found in a dumpster in Washington, DC. My mother, being from right outside DC herself, felt that this was a fitting match for us, and I wasn't about to question her sudden belief in kismet. The adoption application took us hours to complete. We didn't know the first thing about taking care of a puppy and worried we would say something horribly wrong.

Fifteen years later, I'm on the other side of the adoption process, having fostered and adopted out hundreds of dogs and puppies. When it comes to matching a dog with its owner, it's not about first come, first served, or being fair. The fact that a dog needed to be rescued in the first place isn't fair. A good rescue organization is willing to take the time to find the right home for the pup in question. Dogs in rescues and shelters get moved around a lot, and it's our job to ensure that they don't end up back in the overinundated hands of a rescue or shelter.

Make Your Adoption Application Stand Out from the Rest

Here are my tips for making sure your adoption application gets to the top of the pile:

AVOID ONE-WORD ANSWERS. Instead, provide thoughtful replies that show you've done the research and considered all that goes into owning a dog.

PROVE YOU'RE READY TO COMMIT LONG-TERM AND THAT YOU'LL MAKE THIS DOG A PRIORITY. Be specific about your daily schedule. When will you walk the dog? How many times a day? Will you hire a dog walker if you're unable to make time every day?

BE HONEST AND TRANSPARENT. Don't try to hide your work schedule or living situation. Trust that the rescue organization wants you to adopt a dog from them just as much as you want that dog, because remember—it makes space for another dog to be rescued. If your application is promising, a good rescue will try finding a dog that will thrive in your situation, whatever it may be.

SHOW THAT YOU'RE FLEXIBLE. Oftentimes a rescue will give a brief description of a dog on social media, purposely leaving out details on behavioral issues or quirks in fear of scaring away potential adopters. While you may have fallen in love with an Instagram photo of an adorable puppy, the rescue will help you find the perfect match in the end, even if that pup isn't the one you saw in the photo. There are always dogs and pups who haven't been posted yet.

DON'T BE AFRAID TO SHOW YOUR EXCITEMENT AND PASSION. We love that! After all, that shared passion is why we work in rescue.

If you follow these guidelines, hopefully you'll receive an email within the week your application was submitted with next steps toward completing your adoption. GOOD LUCK!

The next morning, we woke up to the best kind of email, with the subject "Adoption approved." The rescue had gotten in touch with our references and was inviting us to the litter's foster home at our earliest convenience. It was like we were being invited to meet the queen. We were finally going to pick out our puppy! My brother and I had never gotten dressed so quickly. The giddiness and excitement were stronger than Chanukah and Christmas combined.

After what felt like the longest morning ever, my family finally arrived at the foster home of seven nearly identical puppies. My brother and I climbed into the pen, not caring about sitting on pee-stained newspapers. The puppies crawled all over us, licking our faces and nipping our ears. I'd done all the research on animal rescue, but I hadn't prepared myself for choosing the right dog (more on that later). While I panicked internally about how to possibly make this grand decision, my little brother had somehow managed to already pick a favorite—a little girl with cartoonish ears bigger than her face that'd crawled into his lap and fell asleep. She chose him, and in turn, he chose her.

Will named the puppy Riley after his preschool girlfriend. Thankfully, Riley the dog lasted much longer than the girlfriend. She was a good girl— sweet yet protective—and after some time, even my parents learned to love this dog. One night, when Riley was a puppy, she got too rambunctious while playing and bit my dad. His hand wouldn't stop bleeding, so he drove the hour from Bedford to New York City in the middle of the night to meet his doctor for a tetanus shot and to glue the bite shut. I was worried that he'd be furious with her. But when I woke up the next morning and saw Dad reading his newspaper and petting Riley's head like nothing had happened, I knew she was here to stay. Now, my dad likes to say that rescues know you saved them and they do what they can to thank you for it. For the twelve years Riley lived, that couldn't have been more true. Every morning started with my dad reading the daily paper over a cup of coffee in

his mustard corduroy recliner. Riley would always paw his leg for him to pet her head, then join him in the recliner next to his. She showed her thanks through constant companionship and affection. She was known for resting her head on your lap and lifting one paw to put in your hand or on your leg without command. She always wanted to stay connected.

Riley's kind demeanor chipped away at my mom's heart, too. Despite being pretty anti-dog, she began to accept Riley as an integral part of our family. A year after adopting her, my mom felt guilty that Riley didn't have a friend. This came as a shock to the rest of my family, but my mom explained that she believed everything and everyone should come in pairs. "That's why we wanted to give you a brother," she told me matter-of-factly, but unlike the six years it took my parents to give me a brother, my mom moved quickly to get one for Riley. That weekend, she informed Will and I that she'd read about a place over the bridge called the North Shore Animal League. Being the Korean-Italian mother she is, she wanted to go right then and there to cross the item off her list and find Riley some company. I thought my mother had absolutely lost her mind. How did she go from wanting no dogs to wanting two dogs so quickly?

Unwilling to wait another day for my dad to return from his business trip, the three of us ventured to the North Shore Animal League that morning in search of a white dog. My mom thought it'd be cute to have one black dog and one white dog. Again, I didn't question her. "Never question Mom" was a lesson well learned early on.

When we arrived at the shelter, I remember thinking, *This place is better than Disneyland!* We hurried through room after room of adorable dogs and puppies wagging their tails and yipping for our attention. Will and I were so excited we could barely contain ourselves. But after nearly an hour of looking, there were no white dogs to be found.

After regrouping, we all agreed on a black pointer-Lab mix with a white spotted chest and booties named Jake. Jake already knew his name and we couldn't agree on a new one, so we decided to keep it. We brought Jake home that same day and introduced him to Riley, excited for what we were sure would be a warm welcome. It wasn't, however, the immediate connection we were hoping for. Riley had little to no interest in Jake, and the feeling was mutual. Riley struggled to share attention, and Jake had no problem trailing off by himself to explore the yard.

FACT
Black dogs are typically chosen last for adoption. Since they stay in shelters the longest, they are more likely to be euthanized than dogs with other colored coats.[1]

Jake 10/14

I'll take another detour here to provide this sidenote: Now that I have more experience with rescue dogs, I've learned that Riley and Jake's lukewarm initial interaction is pretty common. Transitioning another dog into your home isn't always easy, and building a bond between two dogs who have never met takes time. I've seen many dogs returned after only a few weeks because the new dog didn't "get along" with the existing one, and the most frustrating thing is that often the adopter sides with their first dog because

---

1   Emily Friedman, "Prospective Pet Adopters Overlook Black Dogs and Cats, Shelters Say," ABC News, October 9, 2009, https://abcnews.go.com/Technology /AmazingAnimals/pet-owners-overlook-black-dogs-cats-animalshelters/ story?id=8785177

they don't consider the second dog *their* dog yet. Just know that adding another dog to your home not only takes time, but it also makes your dogs equal. Be patient, refer to the plethora of tips and training guides that are available online, or even hire a professional. All right, detour over and done with.

The evening Jake joined our family, we all waited in the driveway for my dad to return from his trip. We were excited to introduce my dad to Jake, but once he arrived and got out of his car, his reaction was *not* what we were expecting: "He's bigger than I thought, and his face is so *pointy*." Ah, my dad's honesty at its finest. Not only was he thrown off by our choice of dog but he also wasn't thrilled with the name Jake. "I feel like this is John Belushi back from the dead to haunt me," he muttered as he came inside. (Belushi played Jake in *The Blues Brothers*. My dad had been his musical director.) My dad thought Jake's white chest and black body resembled the iconic suits the Blues Brothers wore. While this is definitely an observation only my dad would make, I must admit that he wasn't wrong to be skeptical. We quickly learned that, at least initially, Jake was an entirely different kind of dog than Riley. He was possessive of food and toys and would rather have spent his days outside than in the house with our family (this behavior was disappointing at the time, but I've since learned that, for most rescues, it just takes time for them to realize that resources like food and toys are things that are consistently available, so that there's no need to guard them).

Just like Riley biting my dad in the early days, Jake made some big mistakes as well. You see, in addition to Jake and Riley, we also had two bunnies who lived on our back porch in a hut on stilts. They were a gift to Will and me from our parents prior to getting Riley. I think they had hoped these bunnies would satisfy our yearning for a dog. However, just like the glow-in-the-dark fish, the crayfish, the four hermit crabs with *SpongeBob SquarePants* character shells, and the hamster my brother lost (yes, he lost a whole hamster), these bunnies didn't stop us from wanting a dog.

The summer we added Jake to our family, my parents went out one afternoon and left us with our babysitter, Ben. We'd just gotten home from getting pizza when my brother looked out the window and exclaimed, "I think Jake might've got a bird!" Ben and I ran to the window to have a look, glancing at each other wide-eyed. With six years between Will and me, I often felt more like his second mother than his sister growing up, and it was clear to me Jake didn't have a bird. The black-and-white tufts of fur peeking out from his mouth looked sickeningly familiar. Will thankfully hadn't realized that the "bird" was in fact his beloved bunny, Ash (named, of course, after the Pokémon master). I ran outside to try to stop Jake from making it any worse, but Jake became territorial, growling and guarding his prey like a wild animal. It was then that Will put two and two together. I'll never forget looking back and seeing his little sobbing face in the window. I hoped he would never feel that sort of sorrow again.

It took a while for Will to get over the loss of his bunny. Anytime he went anywhere in the house, he would say, "C'mon, Riley—let's go. Jake, I'm not talking to *you*." But with time, Will eventually forgave Jake and came to understand that while dogs are indoor pets, they still have animal instincts. Following that drama, Jake thankfully adjusted and behaved more appropriately. Jake soon settled in and became more comfortable, and at any given time you could look out that same window into the backyard and see Jake and Riley frolicking through the snow, digging holes together, and basking in the sun. They were different yet complementary—Jake began to look up to Riley as an older sister, learning how to behave in a family by following her lead. In turn, Jake showed Riley how to have fun and be more of a rough-and-tumble dog. Thankfully, no more bunnies were consumed during this growing process.

As Riley and Jake became quite attached to each other, we all became quite attached to Riley and Jake. In Riley's later years, my mom would put petroleum jelly on her dry, cracked nose multiple times a day. My dad and I never really thought it helped, but we didn't stop her. We knew it was her way of showing Riley love. Riley didn't grow up to be the Gigi Hadid of dogs. Besides her super dry nose, her legs were short and her belly would sag almost all the way to the ground. Jake was much more buff, even into old age. He remained slim and tall, though his face did get very gray, and my mom would wipe his goopy eyes with a warm, wet paper towel.

As in most families with dogs, my brother and I eventually moved out, leaving my mom and dad to tend to Jake and Riley as they grew old and slowed down. As an empty nester, my mom was always looking for trips to take to distract her from missing us. She even took Jake and Riley to East Hampton to visit Anne. Maysie and I received many photos that weekend of Jake and Riley enjoying the sunset out on the dock while our moms enjoyed their wine. My mom ended up bringing the dogs on many new trips and adventures, just as I do with my dogs. Mothers turn out like their daughters, too.

My mom noticed that Riley was aging at a significantly faster rate than Jake, which was strange since they were only one year apart. She brought Riley to the vet so often the front desk knew the dog by name and had our credit card on file. My mom called me after each appointment, frustrated the vet didn't see what she saw. She was insistent something was wrong, but they just told her it was Riley's old age, prescribing pills to make her comfortable. That winter, my mom found Riley lying in the snow, awake but unmotivated to get up. She was rushed to the twenty-four-hour animal hospital, and my brother met my mom there. They were told that Riley had diabetes *and* cancer. We were all furious this had gone unnoticed by our usual vet after so many visits, but it was too late. We had to do the responsible thing and put her out of her misery.

We buried Riley in the woods surrounding our home and held a ceremony. My family, a few friends, and even our housekeeper and handyman attended and spoke kind words about Riley. We reminisced about her sweet demeanor, her oddly cute cracked nose and sagging belly, and how we would all miss her pawing at our legs to pet her head. She had made an impact on everyone.

Once Riley was gone, Jake declined, too. He'd lost his sister, his best friend, and his mentor. Jake began spending more time indoors with our family. It was like Jake knew he had to fill Riley's void. One night while my dad was out of town, Jake lay at my mom's bedside as she watched her nightly quota of *Law & Order: SVU*. (What do you think of the new season? My mom is disappointed in the episodic storyline.) The next morning when my mom woke up, Jake wasn't outside as he normally was early in the morning (my mom spoiled him with an automatic doggy door). He was still there beside her bed, very quiet and very still. He had passed away that night in his sleep. Mom says Jake died of a broken heart.

We buried Jake next to Riley and held a similar memorial ceremony. Our family was officially dogless, and it stung even for my mom and dad. To answer a question you all might be thinking, no, my parents haven't adopted another dog. Their excuse is that my current dogs—Rue, Echo, and Alfie—are their granddogs now, and also, they want to have the flexibility to visit us on the West Coast and Will at school that dogs wouldn't afford them. But I'm secretly always looking for the perfect dog to travel with them. It'll happen eventually.

The summer before Alfie was born, Rue and Echo joined me on a trip to my hometown of Bedford, New York. It was the first time Rue and Echo had been back since we moved to Los Angeles two years prior. As we were walking in the woods, Rue and Echo sniffed out the spot we had buried Jake and Riley. Brushing away some leaves, I discovered two matching white painted rocks with red hearts that contained Jake's and Riley's names and the years of their lives. I could recognize the handwriting anywhere—it was my mom's. She must've searched for those rocks and painted them herself, because I know my dad wasn't in the woods foraging. I couldn't believe she'd gone to all that trouble, or that she even knew the dates of each of their life spans. Then I remembered that Riley's and Jake's last days were spent mostly with my mom while my dad was working. The sorrow she felt once they were gone made it clear that she had truly bonded with them during that time.

My mom's transformation is a story for anyone who *thinks* they don't like dogs. Though becoming a dog household, we still had rules—no dogs upstairs, no dogs in the kitchen, no dogs in the living room. After ten years of abiding by these rules (despite my brother and me breaking them whenever we were home alone), the dogs eventually earned their freedom to roam the house and then some. Jake slept by my parents' bedside every night until the day he passed.

Shortly after the house became dogless, my mom started volunteering with a local rescue organization, sorting through adoption applications and interviewing applicants. She's now my foster dogs' biggest fan, always calling to check on their progress and donating money when needed. She actually just called to ask what sorts of things she should buy my current two foster dogs and ten foster puppies for Christmas since they will be joining us. Witnessing my mom—a stubborn, hardworking, selfless woman—go from disliking dogs to rooting for them proves the power of a dog's unconditional love and immeasurable companionship.

If you're new to dogs in your life, I hope the stories in this book help win you over like Jake and Riley won over my parents. If, however, you've been obsessed with dogs for at least as long as I have, I hope this book encourages you to consider rescuing and fostering. Lastly, regardless of how long and in what way a dog has been in your life, I hope this book helps you come away with the understanding of a dog's life-changing importance, as well as their magic.

Family portrait

LEARNING THE ROPES

PATIENCE,
PERSISTENCE,
AND PUPPIES

At nineteen I was living in Manhattan, rooming with my parents and attending The New School

(and no, it's not a *new* school; it's a progressive university founded in 1919). I was desperate for a dog of my own, and, as if I were twelve again, I sent links of adoptable puppies to my mother daily. By some grace of God, my mother finally gave in and agreed to cosign adoption papers with me for the most adorable, fits-in-the-palm-of-your-hand Boston terrier–Chihuahua mix.

My dad helped name her Rue, like *street* in French, because, like Riley, she was found on the side of the street in a dumpster (amazing how many dogs are found in dumpsters, isn't it?). Unlike with my family's previous two dogs, I didn't get to meet Rue before

Looking for a name for this 10 week old, 4 pound gal!

officially adopting her, so I knew I had to be flexible and prepared for anything. Rue was being transported from South Carolina to New York along with many other dogs being adopted. The day before we picked her up, I spent an hour at the pet supply store, darting about as I tried to pick out everything I could think of to buy. I wish I could've had this list.

Puppy Necessity Checklist

- ( ) Adjustable collar
- ( ) Tag with puppy name and your contact information
- ( ) Adjustable harness (preferably with front and back D ring)
- ( ) Leash (nonretractable)
- ( ) Poop bag holder and bags
- ( ) Crate with divider panel to expand as he/she grows
- ( ) Something cozy to put in the crate
- ( ) Chew toys, bully sticks, etc. (I recommend the pet aisle at T.J. Maxx)
- ( ) Food and water bowls
- ( ) If you plan on pee-pad training, pee pads and a pad holder with grate to prevent your puppy from shredding the pad
- ( ) Puppy food (ask what your puppy has been eating so you can transition him/her slowly to the food of your choice and not upset his/her stomach)

When I got home from the pet supply store, I paced around my tween brother Will, who was playing video games and actively trying to ignore me and my nervous energy. I was so worried the pink faux leather studded collar I picked out would be too small (for reference, the collar was like a bracelet on my very small and bony wrist). I tossed and turned all night, and at 4:00 a.m., I got a sudden call from the rescue's transport company reporting that the driver was running ahead of schedule. I couldn't get out of bed fast enough.

I burst into my parents' room and woke up my dad. "Get up and get dressed! Rue's coming early!" Panicked that the transport company would see how young I looked and think I was an unfit adopter, I rushed to the bathroom and applied a full face of makeup. While my dad shook off sleep, I put together a mature, professional outfit, like one I would wear for a job interview. My dad was too tired to question the extreme lengths I underwent. We were out of the house in a hurry before the sun even rose, driving toward a train station on the border of New York and Connecticut where we would pick up Rue.

Sometime later, our car rolled into a dark parking lot with just a handful of people in their parked cars waiting. My dad and I fought off yawns as we waited, snuggling into our coats. Our breaths fogged up the windows. Eventually, a big white van pulled into the lot, and everyone got out of their cars and headed over, my dad and I following their lead. It was freezing out. (These miserably cold mornings are the reason I now live in California.) I could barely contain my excitement. We joined the newly formed line, and once I eventually made my way to the front, I handed our adoption form to the driver. He matched the number on the form to a crate jigsawed toward the back, behind even more crates.

"Do you have the girl or the boy?" the driver asked.

"The girl!" I exclaimed.

He smiled, then reached in and pulled out a tiny, scared puppy with a bubble gum pink collar (which I still have to this day). My dad says my eyes lit up when I first saw her. She was cuter than cute. It was exactly what a Jewish kid imagined meeting Santa would be like. When the driver put her frail body in my arms, I realized she was much smaller and balder than she'd looked in her pictures.

The driver suggested I walk Rue to relieve herself since she'd been on the road all night. I pulled the collar I had purchased out of my pocket. I couldn't believe I was worried it would be too small—it was so big it fit around her waist instead of her neck. I attached the recently purchased leash to the collar she was already wearing and tried to walk her, but she just wouldn't budge. I stood there shivering in the brisk early morning air, waiting for her to move, but she never did. After some tugging and pleading, I gave in and picked her up. I wrapped her in a fleece blanket and set her on my dad's lap in the passenger seat of the car, hoping she wouldn't do her business right on his jeans. During that drive home, we realized the rescue hadn't been completely forthcoming about Rue's mental and physical state. Her fur was scarce, eyes crusty, and she was trembling with fear. My dad, remembering the rescue had described her as "a little shy" on Petfinder, said, "This dog isn't shy; she's terrified of the entire world!"

We knew Rue was found with her brother in a dumpster, which is obviously no place for tiny, fragile puppies. However, it was my understanding that the rescue had vetted Rue and nursed her back to health before deeming her adoption-ready, but this did not appear to be the case. After bringing her to her consultation with our new vet, Rue was diagnosed with demodex mites and conjunctivitis. It was going to be a long road to recovery on all levels. For weeks her head was always down, and she would jump at the sound of even a pen dropping. Every time someone came over to the apartment, she'd hide under my bed and refuse to come out, no matter how hard I'd try to coax her. I even hired three trainers with different methods at varying price points, but none of them could get her out from under the bed. They tried to persuade her by throwing cheese, freeze-dried lamb lung, jerky, and even leftover chicken and steak they brought in Ziploc bags from their dinners the night before. I was often unpleasantly surprised when pulling lamb lung off the bottom of my shoe days later. In the training world, these smelly foods are considered "high-quality treats" that are, to a normal dog, impossible to resist. But Rue was too stubborn and scared. Eventually I had to crawl under the bed whenever she went to hide so I could slide Rue out by her two front legs myself.

Like clockwork, each trainer would suggest we try moving outside. I would carry Rue down the hall, into the elevator, and out onto the sidewalk. As instructed, I'd purchased a front-clasping harness and a short leash, but Rue just stood rooted in the middle of the sidewalk. No high-quality treat, special harness, or degree of pulling, dragging, or praising could get this three-pound puppy to move from point A to point B. We got all sorts of glares from people walking by who were clearly annoyed by us blocking the sidewalk, and some were even upset by the sight of an obviously distressed puppy. After several sessions and a ton of money down the drain, the trainers stopped responding to my emails. They had given up on us.

Luckily for Rue, I had no intention of giving up. Of course, this wasn't what I had imagined the first puppy of my adult life would be like, but I was determined to help her. (This quality often leads to disappointment when dating. My dad likes to use the term wounded bird syndrome, which is when someone gravitates toward dating people whom they think they can help and "fix." He clearly thinks I have it.) After mimicking every trainer I hired as well as trainers I watched on YouTube with no success, I disregarded every technique and instead began trusting my gut.

Ever since my brother was born, I've always had a strong maternal instinct, and I let it lead me when it came to Rue. I felt that what she needed was some mega TLC. I hand-fed her, allowed her to sleep cuddled up next to me in bed, and brought her everywhere I could in a doggy hammock slung across my chest. She never left my side. With all this spoiling, Rue slowly started to trust me. She eventually began eating her meals out of a bowl, walking beside me on a leash, and picking up basic commands. Rue's health improved, too. I brought her to the vet for weekly skin scrapes and tests, and I continued to bathe her irritated skin daily with a medical wash and clean her goopy eyes. While probably finding this tedious, Rue was patient and willing. This healing process truly brought her and me closer together. Now, there's rarely Victoria without Rue.

At nine months old, Rue was finally healthy, but she was still struggling to come out of her shell around other people; she still only felt comfortable with me. I so wanted my friends and family to see how adorable, loving, and funny she was behind closed doors, but she was just too shy. Still in college at the time, I'd take my homework to the dog park along the Hudson River in hopes that Rue would meet a dog that would spark some playfulness in her. I've always thought Rue was less like a dog and more like a cat, because nothing she did was very doglike. Instead of playing with other dogs, Rue would sit with me and all the dog owners on the bench, watching the other pups prance about. In winter, she refused to go outside unless she was wearing two layers—a onesie, and either her red wool sweater, plaid fleece, or shearling coat over top. I never thought I would be the sort of person to dress their dog, but Rue insisted on it.

After venting to my mom over the phone about all the trauma Rue had endured in her short little life, she suggested I look into getting Rue a friend, just like we did for Riley. Riley and Jake became very reliant on each other, so maybe the same thing would happen for Rue if I adopted a canine brother. While hopeful at the prospect of some doggy company, the decision to go from one to two was a little daunting. Instead of a comfortable one-to-one ratio, there'd be one of me and two of them, which was a lot of responsibility to shoulder on my own at nineteen. This was a sacrifice I was willing to make, however, if it meant Rue could lead a happier, more confident life.

My friends assured me that if anyone was capable of raising another puppy, it was me. When I got Rue, I had already relinquished the expected college privileges of staying out late and sleeping in, so it wasn't as if I'd be missing out on much. After a short time to think about it, I decided to take the plunge and look for another puppy to adopt. I'd convinced myself that since I was already struggling through the puppy phase with Rue, adding a second puppy now would save me the trouble of reliving this chaos and exhaustion again in the future. I told anyone who doubted my plan (including myself during the toughest of times), "A year from now, I'll have two potty-trained dogs who sleep through the night, and we'll all be cruising through life."

DIY
Learning the Ropes

Repurpose Old Linens into New Toys

As a college student raising two puppies, I often had to find creative ways to save money on pet supplies. Making your own rope toy is a great, easy way to repurpose old linens instead of throwing them away. All you need are scissors, fabric, and the ability to do a standard braid.

Alfie & his favorite rope toy

Cut your fabric into three strips and braid the strips together, knotting both ends. You can experiment by mixing and matching linens and textures and playing around with lengths and thicknesses. I love making long, chunky ropes by braiding three ropes out of different linens and then braiding all three together. It's also fun to play around with knots! You can make your "rope" into a ring shape or even add "beads" by using dog toys with holes in them already, or by cutting a hole straight through a tennis ball. The possibilities are endless!

These rope toys are scattered all over my house, and they've become the favorites of Rue, Echo, Alfie, and all my foster dogs. They're environmentally friendly, washable, and beat any store-bought toy. Give it a try—and a tug!

Three

TAKE A PAWS

❖

FOSTERING IS NOT FOR THE FAINT OF HEART

Fostering is the most selfless thing a person can do in the rescue world.

It's far more work than just caring for your own dogs. You have to be strong, and your own dogs have to be strong. It's not always easy for Rue, Echo, and Alfie to share my attention and their space with all the dogs in and out of our home. It's a major sacrifice that requires a ton of patience. A major part of fostering is helping your foster dogs overcome behavioral issues and trauma or handling health and medical needs before they're ready for adoption. Despite the amount of work, sleepless nights, and frustrating mornings, watching your foster dog transform and grow is incredibly rewarding. You're only human; you get attached and it is difficult to see them go. I always say you can't keep them all, but you can try to save them all.

The Charcuterie litter

I've been fostering since 2012. At that time, I was living at my parents' apartment on the Upper West Side. I'd just adopted Rue and my world was turned upside down by all that she'd been through. I wanted to do more. My first foster puppies were from what I would now consider an irresponsible rescue. Once, while I was on my way home from school during my sophomore year of college, I stopped by the two-story Petco in Union Square to pick up supplies for Rue. They were hosting an adoption event out front for a rescue organization. The next thing I knew, I was bringing home two chow mix brothers, one black and one tan. There was no home check done beforehand, and looking back, I don't recall even filling out any paperwork, either. The lack of these security checks is a telltale sign of an irresponsible rescue, the kind that'll pawn off tiny puppies to a college student about whom they know nothing.

FACT

Young puppies are often sent to foster homes in pairs. It's much easier (and quieter) to care for them when they have a partner to cuddle with and entertain each other.

Nevertheless, I headed for the subway with the dog carrier they'd given me slung over my shoulder. Down the stairs and underground we went. While waiting for the train, I sat down on the bench with the carrier set by my side. For the first time, I got a good look at them through the mesh siding of the bag—two little cotton balls looking around with wide-eyes. I really couldn't have gotten a cuter pair as my first fosters.

We got a lot of attention riding uptown, and I was already handing out my number to those interested in adopting them. Considering the unexpected nature of my first foster arrangement, my dad (who several nights out of the week, depending on his schedule, stayed in our NYC apartment) was about to be *very* surprised when he got home from work. I quickly set up a makeshift puppy den for them in my little brother's bathroom before my dad arrived to make it look like I had things under control. Luckily, I already had puppy pads, a bed, toys, and kibble of Rue's to spare.

Fostering Puppies Supply List

Fostering can have a lot of twists and turns. Illness can arise, behavioral issues, and so forth—if you can think of it, it can happen. The purpose of a foster home is to see how a dog acts in a home so the rescue organization can get a better idea of who might be the perfect adopter and what kind of home environment would be the right one. Since this is likely the first time the dog is living in a proper home, you don't know much going into it; therefore, a good foster should be ready for anything. Gather these supplies if you're thinking about fostering litters of puppies:

○ Empty baby pool for inside your home. Puppies will sleep and nurse in here cozy with linens until they can climb out. This makes for a much easier way for mama to access her puppies and keep track of them.

○ Playpen

○ Towels, sheets, blankets

○ Tarp, baby "splat mat" or plastic drop cloth, or an easy-to-clean / nonabsorbent floor

○ Bottles

○ Paper towels or rags

○ Milk replacer/formula

○ Dyne

○ Puppy kibble

○ Puppy canned/wet food

○ Blender

○ Large food and water bowls for mama

○ Cupcake tin (designate one cupcake-size bowl in tin for each puppy) or shallow cake pan for feeding

○ Shallow water bowl for puppies

○ Heating pad or hot water bottle

○ Cardboard or fencing to build boundary wall at entryway of puppy pen so that the puppies can't climb out, but mama can still jump in

○ Kitchen scale

○ Bowl large enough to fit a puppy in (this will go on top of the kitchen scale; don't forget to zero out your scale when the bowl is on top!)

○ Custom weight chart

○ Weaning puppy collars

○ Collar with ID tag for mama

NOTE: A good rescue will offer to provide necessary supplies, but if you want to go a step above, donating/buying these supplies for your own foster to have them on hand won't go unnoticed and will make your life easier!

After setting up the foster chow puppies' area, I let Rue out of her crate. She traced the smells to the puppies without hesitation. She glared at them, then up at me with a look like, *Who the hell are these guys?* Little did she know that these guys would be the first of many, many foster siblings she'd have.

While getting acquainted with our new houseguests, I discovered to my dismay that the puppies were infested with fleas. When parting their long hair, you could see little black dots crawling all over their skin like a bunch of kids hyped up on candy corn in a corn maze. The fleas were even in and around their eyes. While I was upset that the rescue had let them live with such an extreme case of fleas under their care, I wasn't about to return the puppies, as I was worried they would continue to be neglected. I immediately called the rescue I'd gotten them from in fear I'd put Rue in harm's way (not to mention the fear that my parents' furniture would be infested with fleas forever). The rescue seemed unfazed by my concern.

I recruited some friends to help me scrub the fosters with flea shampoo and Dawn dish soap (Dawn dish soap and other soaps like it suffocate the fleas on the skin). Combing out dead fleas with the tiny flea comb seemed to be an endless task, and my friends were heroes that day for helping.

Hero #1: Gabby

Hero #2: Sam

Knowing my dad would be coming home soon, I ran out to grab us some dinner. Though I don't support his Coca-Cola addiction, I bought him his favorite Mexican Coke in a glass bottle to butter him up. When my dad arrived, he greeted Rue with the love and affection he always does no matter how many times he comes home to her pee on the carpet.

"I have a surprise for you," I said.

"Uh-oh, what is it?"

I took out a chilled bottle. "A Mexican Coke!"

He smiled, looking relieved. "My favorite!" he said, taking it from my hand. "Thank you." He cracked off the bottle cap, poured it over a glass of ice, and took a sip. "Ah, delicious!"

"That's not the only surprise I have for you," I said hesitantly, plastering on a big smile.

He paused. "Uh-oh, what is it?" he asked again.

Why is it that whenever you tell someone you have a surprise for them, they say, "Uh-oh"? I guided him into my brother's room and opened the bathroom door to reveal the two cotton balls fast asleep behind the toilet. I crossed my fingers in the hopes their cuteness would win him over. After all, there's nothing cuter than sleeping, snuggling puppies.

"What?!" he exclaimed. Not in the mad type of way, exactly—more in the "How did *this* happen?" kind of way. As he looked at me exasperatedly, I told him the story: after helping Rue overcome her trauma, I wanted to do more, and after the flea infestation, there was no way I could send them back. I promised to keep them off the carpets and take good care of them, and after my hard sell, he kindly agreed to let them stay.

"I already have one puppy," I told him, giving Rue a scratch behind her ears. "What difference does two more make?" Famous last words.

Next, it was time to convince my mother. My mom rarely came into the city since she had to stay back in Bedford while my brother attended school. My dad and I tag teamed her over the phone, easing into the conversation with a topic we knew she'd enjoy, complimenting her and agreeing to do whatever it was she needed (this usually consists of cleaning or organizing something), and then hitting her with the big question we hoped she would say yes to. This is a trick we've been doing for the past twenty-plus years. (For example, this is how we convinced her we needed state-of-the-art massage chairs from Brookstone. When my dad was doing a residency at Caesars Palace in Vegas, the two of us used to sit in them during his lunch breaks and made the entire family try them out.) Mom wasn't thrilled about having three puppies in the apartment with a wall-to-wall mural carpet, but after assuring her I'd find the chows new homes soon, they were allowed to stay. The apartment quickly turned into what looked like the baby gate showroom at Buy Buy Baby, and as a person who's not quite five foot two, I hoped I wouldn't have to straddle these tension baby gates soon, too.

I was so proud when I found a woman and her friend willing to adopt my fosters. Seeing how excited these women were to adopt their first puppies together and how thankful they were for all my hard work gave me the foster bug. Eight years later, my house is like my very own little shelter with, at times, up to fifteen dogs and puppies. I never get sick of seeing people's faces light up on adoption day. It's what makes it all worth it.

PUP CULTURE

Bob Letterman

BOB AND DAVID LETTERMAN

This is a story about my first dog. His name was Bob. Like anybody with a dog, and maybe even more so with the first dog, you don't understand how much you will love and care for and worry about the dog. The other thing is, you don't understand that the personality an animal has will be far greater than you imagine.

I found Bob in the San Fernando Valley. He was in a nightclub called the SHOW-BIZ, which was not far from where I lived. If you were a comedian or a singer or a musician, you could go to the SHOW-BIZ almost any night, and if they had time, they would let you go up on stage and you could do your comedy or your songs, your music—whatever you wanted to do. They also had a kitchen at the SHOW-BIZ where they served meals, or at least food. It wasn't Caesars Palace. It was not like Mohegan Sun. It was a little run-down, but it was pleasant enough and people would go there, and you'd have an audience.

One night I was waiting to go on and I just kind of looked into the kitchen to see what manner of health violations were on display, and there was this dog eating a cheeseburger off the kitchen floor. I thought, "Well, that's, you know . . . that's kind of *interesting*." I'd not seen that before. I watched the dog eat the cheeseburger, and then he finished up and he sort of just wandered around the nightclub. I asked people, "Does he belong to someone working in the kitchen? Is there a man or a woman who owns this dog? Is he going on stage?" The answer was always no. The back door to the club had been open, and I was told that the dog wandered in from the parking lot and found his way into the kitchen, and they made him a cheeseburger. Believe me—I've never in my entire life had that kind of luck, where I just wandered into a place and somebody handed me a cheeseburger.

I took a liking to the dog. He looked a little like a Belgian shepherd but not as big, maybe two-thirds the size of the Belgian shepherd. More like a Luxembourg shepherd. No collar, no tag, no ID, no nothing. That night when I left the club, I put the dog in the car with me and took him back to my house. The next day I drove him around the neighborhood, trying to find out where his home was. Everywhere I went, nobody knew him; they'd never seen him around—*He's not ours*, *We don't know*, *He's a stranger* . . . on and on and on. Satisfied that he was indeed a stray, I took him to the vet. The vet checked him out and the poor thing had worms. They had to deworm him—and by the way, I will say the dog and I had that in common.

He became my dog, and I named him Bob because he just looked like a dog named Bob. The YMCA in my neighborhood was giving dog-training lessons every Tuesday and Thursday, so Bob and I signed up. I had nothing to do because I was working at night, so I'd take Bob to the training lessons. I taught Bob to sit and to stay, to heel and to come, and he got to be pretty good at it. Certainly, better at it than I was. As everybody knows, the more time you spend with your animal, the deeper and tighter the bond becomes, and Bob was my good friend for years and years and years.

Once, Bob and I spent Thanksgiving at my girlfriend's house. The day before Thanksgiving, she and I placed our frozen turkey on the kitchen counter to thaw, and we went out to do the rest of our Thanksgiving shopping. We were gone for forty-five minutes, maybe an hour. We came back, and it's now, "Where'd you put the turkey?" She said, "Well, it was right here," and I said, "Oh, well, let's look around." And it was one of those things where you check it a hundred times because you can't believe what was there has now vanished, especially in forty-five minutes. We're now at the point where we're confounded, and we can't explain it. The only logical explanation seemed to be that someone broke into the house, saw the turkey and maybe needed the turkey to eat, and helped him- or herself to the turkey and left. We thought, *Okay, well, if somebody who needed the food got the food, then that's fine. It's Thanksgiving. We'll go get another turkey.* This time we just kept it in the refrigerator to thaw.

The next day we get up and put the new turkey in the oven. After about an hour, as you know if you've ever cooked a turkey, the house filled up with the lovely aroma. So, we're an hour in and we hear something banging around by the back door. We opened the door and there was Bob with the original turkey, semifrozen and covered in mud (the turkey, not Bob). And by the way, we had filed a missing turkey report.

Bob had somehow knocked the fifteen-pound turkey off the counter, dragged it across the floor, let himself out the door, took it into the backyard, and buried it. Luckily, he hadn't killed himself with the thing. The next day when he smelled the turkey cooking in the house, he brought his turkey in, and I said to myself, "If I live to be a thousand, I'll never witness anything this magical again." That day became my Thanksgiving miracle, thanks to my good boy Bob, who to this day I still love to pieces. That's the end of my story.

— *David Letterman*

Foods and Plants Your Dog Should Stay Away From

Not every dog will have access to an entire frozen turkey to steal like Bob, so here's some advice from Dr. Gary Weitzman, DVM, president and CEO of San Diego Humane Society (and author of eight books), about other foods and plants that dogs, in general, should stay away from. If your dog gets into any one of these foods, contact organizations like the ASPCA Animal Poison Control Center, the national Pet Poison Helpline, or your friendly neighborhood veterinarian. And remember: try not to leave a whole turkey out for your dog to bury.

DR. WEITZMAN: Pets are always eating things they shouldn't. It's important to know the deadliest toxins to prevent a tragedy. Lock chemicals and medications away in cabinets, remove dangerous plants and flowers from your home and yard, keep trash cans secured with lids or stowed under cabinets, don't leave household or automobile fluids lying around, and avoid feeding foods that are toxic to pets. Toxins can act fast. Don't delay seeking veterinary treatment if you think your pet has ingested something poisonous. Timely treatment might be the difference between life and death.

FOODS

Some foods aren't safe for pets because of their metabolic and physiological differences from us. Some can cause organ inflammation or even failure. Don't feed your pet the following:

Alcohol	**Garlic (okay only in small amounts)**	**Rhubarb**
Apple seeds		**Stone fruit pits**
Avocado	**Grapes and raisins**	**Tea**
Chocolate (especially dark chocolate)	**Macadamia nuts**	**Tomato leaves**
	Moldy foods	**Walnuts**
Coffee	**Onions**	
Dough with yeast	**Potato (raw)**	

If your pet eats a large quantity of any food on this list, it's critical you take him or her to your vet or emergency clinic. With prompt treatment and supportive care, often with IV fluids and observation, most pets will recover.

PLANTS

Many plants and flowers are toxic to pets. Given their propensity for chewing on plants, cats are at the most risk for plant toxicity. Many plants are irritants, meaning they'll cause vomiting, inappetence, and diarrhea. Some also cause inflammation of the mouth, leading to itchiness and swelling. Certain others affect particular organs and might cause difficulty breathing, drooling, irregular heartbeat, or excessive drinking and urinating. When you go to your vet, bring the plant sample along with you. The following are common dangerous plants and flowers. For a complete list, visit www.aspca.org and search "toxic plants."

Autumn crocuses

Azaleas

Cyclamens

Daffodils

Dieffenbachias

Dracaenas

Hyacinths

Kalanchoes (mother-in-law plant)

Lilies (tiger, day, Asiatic, Easter, and Japanese show lilies)

Lilies of the valley

Oleanders

Philodendrons

Sago palms

Tulips

ALCOHOL

Alcohol can poison a pet by ethanol toxicity. The problem with ethanol toxicity is that varying amounts of a poison might cause problems in different pets. Anything that contains ethanol is toxic to pets, including rum cake, mouthwash, cough medicine, unbaked bread dough (due to the fermenting yeast), and even rotten apples. Play it safe and keep all "over twenty-one" beverages out of your pet's reach. Signs of poisoning include weakness and lethargy, lack of coordination, and drowsiness leading to unconsciousness. Left untreated, the toxicity can lead to heart attack and death. With quick treatment, most animals recover within about a day.

ANTIFREEZE OR HYDRAULIC FLUID

Ethylene glycol poisoning, which occurs when pets ingest antifreeze or hydraulic fluid, is sadly quite common. Pets frequently encounter antifreeze when it leaks from a car onto the garage floor. This bright-green liquid has a sweet taste. Pets might take a lick to investigate or might walk through the antifreeze, then lick it off their paws. Just a few licks can do irreversible damage to the kidneys. Immediate symptoms of antifreeze poisoning are very much like alcohol toxicity. They include drooling and vomiting, uncoordinated or wobbly movement (seems "drunk"), head tremors, increased drinking and urination, muscle twitching, and depression. As time passes, symptoms progress to include decreased drinking but increased urination, low body temperature, extreme lethargy or coma, and seizures. Untreated ethylene glycol poisoning, even in very small amounts, is fatal in dogs. If you even suspect your dog might have ingested this, seek medical care immediately. When caught early enough (within about five hours of ingestion), most dogs will recover uneventfully within a few days of intensive care in the hospital. In cases of delayed treatment, the kidneys might fail.

MARIJUANA AND CBD

Veterinarians in the United States are seeing more cases of marijuana poisoning in pets as more states legalize or decriminalize the drug. Pets can become intoxicated by inhaling secondhand smoke or eating marijuana—either the plant itself or food items containing the drug. Symptoms include incoordination, disorientation, hyperactivity, unusual or increased vocalization, drooling, uncontrolled urination, muscle tremors, seizures, and even coma. In rare cases, pets have died after ingesting large amounts of the psychoactive ingredient in marijuana, tetrahydrocannabinol (THC).

With less toxic potential, cannabidiol (CBD) is the other half of the marijuana equation. CBD is currently marketed without veterinary approval with claims that it can treat everything from joint pain to anxiety and even cancer in dogs. We don't know everything about its potential in dogs, and solid research is needed before veterinary approval to use it in our animals. Diagnosis is heavily reliant on self-reporting, and many pet owners are reluctant to self-report. We can test for THC levels in the urine, but these tests take too long and are impractical, so an honest history of exposure is critical. Once that's established, vets can make an effective treatment plan. Fortunately, most symptoms are short-lived and resolve quickly in pets.

MUSHROOMS

Mushrooms are among the most poisonous of organics. Signs of mushroom toxicity vary depending on the type and amount of mushroom ingested. Some cause simple gastrointestinal distress, others affect the nervous system, and still others can lead to liver or kidney failure. The most common symptoms are weakness, vomiting and diarrhea, jaundice, drooling, and abdominal pain. Seizures and coma can also occur. If you suspect your dog ate an unsafe mushroom, go immediately to your vet or emergency clinic and bring a sample of the mushroom. The mushroom can be submitted for identification, but treatment should not be delayed while waiting for this information. With treatment, prognosis is usually good, although particularly toxic mushrooms have a more difficult prognosis dependent entirely on how quickly you can get your pet to the vet.

Four

THE
CONE OF
SHAME

❧

OVERCOMING
MEDICAL MALADIES

When Rue was nine months old,

I revisited my old friends petfinder.com and adoptapet.com to adopt my second dog. I scrolled through them every day—multiple times a day—to find new puppies the minute they were posted. Unfortunately, I wasn't selected for many of the listings I applied to because of my age. I specifically remember being heartbroken after being denied a white pit bull mix with a black spot around one eye that reminded me of the dog from my favorite childhood movie, *Cheaper by the Dozen*. But then, I thought of the advice I now give to adopters who can't decide which pup to choose: "A month from now you're not going to think back and say, 'I wish we got that *other* dog.' You're going to choose your dog today, fall in love tomorrow, and never look back." And it was true: one day Echo was listed, and I never looked back. It may sound cheesy, but I do believe Echo was meant to be my dog. His goofy grin and wet nose wake me every morning. He sup-

ported and guided me on the dimly lit streets of New York; he protects me from eerie sounds in my house when I'm all alone. He loves me unconditionally—even when I won't give him a second bully stick no matter how much of a fuss he makes. (Those things are expensive, and we already go through a bag a week!)

THE CONE OF SHAME

THE CONE OF SHAME   **43**

Echo had only one slightly blurry photo on his adoptapet.com profile, but his muddy white fluffy coat, speckled ears, piercing green-blue eyes, and milk chocolate brown nose pushing through a chain-link fence caught my attention. He was the most beautiful puppy I had ever seen (sorry, Rue). I FaceTimed my parents to show him off. They were skeptical.

"He's beautiful," they said. "But he looks like he'll be big . . ."

"No, no," I assured them. "His description says he's a mini Australian shepherd mix and that he'll only be thirty pounds. That's the perfect size!"

If I'm being completely honest, the only downside of rescuing a puppy is that you can't know for certain the breed, size, or history of the dog you're adopting. Who remembers the Wonder Ball? For those that don't, it was a hollow chocolate ball filled with a surprise candy and prize inside. Bear with me—this is a bizarre attempt at a metaphor for adopting a puppy from a '90s kid. As you chip away at your puppy's metaphorical chocolate shell, you'll learn about your puppy's personality and the effects of any formative trauma from their past. (Isn't it crazy that a rescue puppy can already have a past in their short little life?) As you watch them grow, you might discover a surprising size or an unexpected trauma response, but no matter what, you'll have a truly worthwhile prize—your dog's unconditional love, companionship, and quirky personality you just can't imagine living without.

Rescues try to make an educated guess based on many factors, including parents' size and look (if known), paw size, rate of growth, and past experience, but oftentimes adopters still end up surprised with their pup. If you're a good dog owner, by the time your puppy is fully grown, size, quirks, and looks don't matter because you've already fallen in love. In Echo's case, I was very surprised, but in the best way possible. I fell in love.

Within forty-eight hours of applying, I was approved to adopt Echo, and my parents cosigned his adoption papers. That weekend, my mom and I drove to a gas station in New Jersey to meet the transport service driving him up from Georgia. (It can all happen so fast.) This transport van was not as official as the one that delivered Rue. This was a beat-up minivan with three puppies loose in the back surrounded by feces and puke.

The driver slid open the van door and there was Echo, filthy yet still stunning in my eyes. I reached in to pick him up and could feel skin and bones underneath all that mud-coated, cotton candy–like fur. I carried him back to our car to meet Rue, but she snapped at him immediately. It wasn't exactly the welcome I was hoping for, but after Riley and Jake's initial interaction, I'd learned to have low expectations. The drive home was a bit of a mess: Echo threw up all over the car. Little did I know that I'd be cleaning up Echo's bodily secretions for the next year.

Soon after bringing Echo home, I discovered he was very sick. You see, he was the biggest food-hog of a dog I'd ever met, but he was allergic to almost *everything* he loved—cheese, chicken, rice: a.k.a. dairy, poultry, and even grains. New York City's streets were Echo's stomach's worst nightmare. He would lunge toward every night-old dollar-slice pizza on the curb; he'd peck at granules of halal-stand rice sprinkled across the sidewalk as if he were a pigeon. He never cared about the pain and suffering that followed.

It was very difficult raising a food-motivated puppy with allergies. He, of course, didn't care what he was allergic to, and he couldn't tell me when his stomach was upset. A lot of frustrated, sleep-deprived tears were shed as I spent most nights cleaning up after him, hauling bags of soiled towels to the trash chute while still half asleep. On the rare occasion when I woke before he became ill, we'd run outside as quickly as we could, usually to no avail. We didn't always make it in time.

One night, after recently moving into my first apartment in Chelsea, Echo and I were rushing outside for another bathroom emergency when we ran into a neighbor waiting for the elevator. Unrealistically tall, dark, and handsome, this neighbor had caught my eye and the eyes of my friends on several previous occasions. Each time we'd spot him, they'd stare and ask, "Who in the world is THAT and why don't we know him?" Here I was, *finally* having crossed paths with this mysterious good-looking man in my building! I tried to play it cool. We made small talk while waiting for the elevator, the numbers above the elevator doors going up and up and up. While we waited, I introduced him to Echo.

He smiled dazzlingly. "He's so cute!" he gushed.

I tried to hide my giddiness. I've always believed that a dog was a single person's best wing(wo)man, and I thought that was the case this time. But boy was I wrong. At that very instant, Echo just couldn't hold it anymore. The face the handsome man made as Echo squatted to relieve himself was cringeworthy in its own right. Remember Maya Rudolph's graphic bathroom break from that horribly disgusting scene in *Bridesmaids*? Yep, that was Echo. Without saying another word, leading-man neighbor stepped into the elevator, leaving me with a mess on the hallway carpet and embarrassment as deep as the hole in Echo's stomach.

Desperate for answers, I brought Echo back to the vet. The vet told me that white dogs were more prone to sensitivities (for example, sunburn) than black or brown dogs, and that it would just take time to figure out what upset Echo's stomach (I also ask Dr. Gary Weitzman about this in chapter 11). Besides Echo's inability to potty train, he was still skin and bones. My dad often told me half-jokingly, "We have to figure out how to put some weight on this dog. People are going to think we starve him." Echo's allergies and sensitive stomach made finding kibble that agreed with him extremely difficult. Through trial and error, and bags and bags of kibble, I finally found a limited-ingredient, grain-free, lamb-based kibble that worked for him, and we stuck with it for years.

🐾
FACT
Most large pet supply stores, like Petco or PetSmart, have an understanding return policy that ensures customers can return an opened bag of kibble if their dog won't eat it or is allergic. Ask about your local store's policy if you're unsure your pet will like the kibble you purchase.

I hauled twenty-seven-pound bags of this kibble from the Petco in Union Square to my apartment on Twentieth Street and Sixth Avenue twice a month. Let me tell you, there's no feeling more gross and irritating than sweating underneath your wool sweater and winter coat in seven-degree weather. It's so itchy! Eventually I resorted to a granny cart for help, and Rue often hitched a ride. See the kibble underneath Rue?

Because of Echo's inability to keep food down and put on weight, his energy was too inconsistent to bring him to puppy school, so we fell behind on his training. When Echo was about nine months old, I eventually signed us up for a basic obedience course highly regarded in New York City. This was my first time attending a group training class, as it was never an option with shy, traumatized Rue.

We arrived on the first day to find that every other dog was the size of Echo's head. During free-play time, the teacher asked me to keep Echo leashed for the teacup-size dogs' safety. It didn't matter that Echo wouldn't hurt a fly—his size spooked most of the dog owners in the class. After week two, the tables had turned—Echo was one of the few dogs allowed off leash. He had proven that despite the judgment put upon him for his size, he was the gentlest dog there. The class nicknamed him "the gentle giant," and he graduated with flying colors and a lot of miniature new friends.

To my surprise, the rescue had estimated only one-third of Echo's final body weight. Full grown and healthy, Echo is now a whopping ninety pounds. Since stabilizing Echo on the limited-ingredient food, the FDA came out with a study saying that grain-free food causes fatal health problems like heart disease and cancer in dogs. Knowing that Echo had grown out of most of his food allergies and no longer had difficulty putting on weight (he was now teetering on being overweight), I tried to switch him to a healthy grain-based kibble. To my relief, the grains didn't upset his stomach, but they did irritate his skin. Since the age of three, Echo has been prone to hot spots.[2] A terrible hot spot on his back right leg soon turned into a granuloma,[3] which to this day has been the death of me (for anyone counting, that's the past six years). If only he would stop licking it!

For a long time, I thought the rest of Echo's life would be spent in a cone, constantly rotating between vet visits and racing outside before something came out of him I did *not* want to clean up. No allergy shots, pills, sprays, or washes have ever made the granuloma go away for good, and unfortunately, because of the location of the granuloma, a skin graft isn't an option. As I write this, Echo isn't wearing the cone, but he's certainly testing it. My friends all know not to be startled when I scream, "Echo!" out of nowhere. "His leg?" they ask, as if there's any other answer. There's nothing more frustrating than your dog not understanding that if they would just stop doing something, their life would be so much easier.

---

2 **Hot spots:** Red, inflamed, and itchy spots on the skin. Oftentimes, the puss entices the dog to lick and scratch, making it difficult to keep dry and heal.

3 **Granuloma:** Referred to as a lick granuloma, it typically appears after a hot spot from excessive licking. Many believe the excessive licking to be a compulsive disorder. As in Echo's case, most granulomas are found on a dog's legs, making it nearly impossible for them to heal properly and avoid bacterial infection. Brushing up against grass and still being accessible even with a cone make for a constant battle.

Common Dog Ailments

There are many ailments that affect dogs each year, especially if they've been on the street for a while. Below is a list of common ailments that affect dogs, ranging from the mild to the severe, from Banfield Pet Hospital's 2019 State of Pet Health Report.[4] If you have a pup of your own, be sure to always take your furry friend to the vet for routine checkups so they can live long, healthy lives.

INTESTINAL PARASITES 508 cases per 10,000

FLEAS AND TICKS 506 cases per 10,000

ARTHRITIS 450 cases per 10,000

ENVIRONMENTAL ALLERGY (ATOPY)
357 cases per 10,000

FLEA ALLERGY 179 cases per 10,000

DENTAL DISEASE 77 cases per 100

HEARTWORM 54 cases per 10,000

KIDNEY DISEASE 50 cases per 10,000

DIABETES MELLITUS 38 cases per 10,000

OVERWEIGHT/OBESITY 31 cases per 100

FOOD ALLERGY 19 cases per 10,000

OTITIS EXTERNA (SWIMMER'S EAR) 16 cases per 100

---

4   https://www.banfield.com/state-of-pet-health

Echo and I have now settled on a healthy-weight food; he eats grain-free kibble instead of the limited-ingredient staple, and this has worked well for us. There are so many varying opinions and studies out there about what to feed your dog, but I think owning a dog is like parenting—everyone critiques the way other people do it, giving unprompted advice about what works for them. Other dog owners always told me how I should be training Rue and what I should be feeding Echo. They may have had their doubts about nineteen-year-old me and my ability to go to school, work, and raise two time-consuming puppies in New York City, but I proved them wrong. Listen to your gut, trust your instincts, and figure out what's best for you and your dog. Like children, every dog is different!

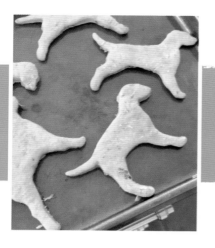

Echo's Favorite Healthy Homemade Dog Biscuits

This dog biscuit recipe I created uses cinnamon as a natural anti-inflammatory. Cinnamon is also good for a dog's brain in small amounts. The parsley helps digestion and fights bad breath, and the peanut butter is high in protein and vitamins B and E. Feel free to use this recipe as a starting point and be creative in combining ingredients your dog will like and benefit from.

WHAT YOU'LL NEED

- 1 cup peanut butter (make sure there's no xylitol in the ingredients, as it's toxic to dogs)
- 1 egg
- 2 teaspoons honey
- 1 cup water
- 4 cups whole wheat flour, divided
- 1 teaspoon baking powder
- 1 teaspoon cinnamon
- 2 teaspoons fresh or dried parsley

1 Preheat the oven to 350 degrees Fahrenheit. Line a baking sheet with parchment paper.

2 Mix the peanut butter, egg, honey, and water in a large bowl.

3 Add 2 cups of the whole wheat flour, the baking powder, cinnamon, and parsley. Continue adding the rest of the flour slowly, until you reach a dough consistency (you may need more or less, depending on your peanut butter).

4 Once your dough has formed, take it out of the bowl and knead it on a clean, flour-dusted surface. Roll your dough out and cut your biscuits using a cookie cutter of your choice.

5 Place the biscuits on the prepared baking sheet. Bake for 20 minutes. Let cool before serving to your dog or storing in your refrigerator in an airtight container for up to two weeks.

Chigger, courtesy of Glenn Close

CHIGGER AND GLENN CLOSE

One day, when I was shooting the first *Sarah, Plain and Tall* in central Kansas, a skinny, traumatized dog appeared at the door of my camper. We were shooting on the outskirts of a small town, in the middle of the prairie. The dog's mangy coat was shockingly matted, and he had so many ticks on him I marveled that he had any blood left at all. He had chosen my camper out of all the other vehicles in our base camp. It was a sign. So, I took him to the nearest vet where they cleaned him up and discovered he was dangerously malnourished, dehydrated, and suffering from dreaded heartworm. Back with us, in the motel and on set, we concluded that he must have existed mainly on insects because he kept snapping them out of the air and munching them down—even wasps—so we named him Chigger. He came back east with us, was mercifully cured of heartworm, and became a beautiful, adored

**Chigger and Annie,
courtesy of Glenn Close**

addition to our family. He never was the bravest of boys, but he patiently let four-year-old Annie dress him in all kinds of getups, and he never complained when she even staged a rather elaborate wedding between him and bossy little Belle, our female border terrier. He lived out his life sitting on our back porch, snapping up insects all summer long, having to be cajoled back inside—always afraid to get too far from home. He started failing after Annie left for college, and he now lies next to Belle, Gaby, Jake, Bill, Eve, and Rainbow, under a row of fragrant viburnum bushes. Every time I have to get on a plane, I imagine that he is in my special pack of four-legged guardian angels, calmly sitting on the wing, just outside my window, looking at me with his soulful gaze, eternally ready to come to my rescue.

—Glenn Close

MUTT SCOUTS

UNLEASHING THE
TRUE HEROES

There are plenty of people in rescue for the wrong reasons.

These individuals are often preoccupied by their image; they hope to get connected with A-listers, and they might even pocket money for themselves. I've been fostering dogs and puppies for nine years now, and unfortunately, I've worked with a lot of questionable rescues. As you learned in chapter 3, my very first fostering experience was with a rescue that gave me two flea-infested puppies on a whim with no interview or paperwork. To further my point, I'm going to share a doozy of a story—one that's purposely vague for legal reasons. (Yup, get ready to buckle in! I told you—it's a doozy.) Last year, a friend of mine found a dog wandering the streets. For the sake of this story, let's call this dog Spot and my friend Doris. Doris called me asking what to do with the stray dog she'd found, and I said, "Give me an hour to find a foster home."

Upon seeing Spot's photo, I realized I knew the perfect person to foster-to-adopt—he'd been looking to adopt this particular breed and would be ecstatic at the opportunity to help rescue her. For those new to the rescue world, foster-to-adopt is when a dog isn't ready to be officially adopted—whether due to behavioral or medical reasons, or, in Spot's case, if it's a stray that therefore needs to be put on "stray hold."

You see, legally, when a dog is found as a stray, nobody can adopt it until it's been listed as lost for two weeks, in hopes of reuniting it with the original owner. And I was right: the person I hoped would care for Spot while on stray hold was more than excited to take her. I called Doris to make the arrangements, but I quickly learned she'd grown impatient and anxious about Spot. As it turns out, Doris panicked and dropped Spot off at a local groomer that doubled as a rescue. Scrambling, I called this local groomer and rescue and introduced myself and my background, assuring them I had someone who would love to foster-to-adopt Spot. They said they had no idea who Spot was and had no recollection of a dog being dropped off that even fit my description. At a loss, I left my phone number, hoping someone more knowledgeable could call me back with good news.

The next morning, I received a call from the head of the rescue who said she'd heard I had information on Spot's owner. I explained that I did not, but that instead I'd found a foster home for her. She then informed me (in no uncertain terms) that Spot was staying at *their* kennels and that we'd have to look for updates on their social media pages like everyone else.

It made zero sense. Why would a small rescue prefer to keep a dog in a kennel when a loving, comfortable foster home was available? Every day my friend wanting to foster-to-adopt and I checked their social media pages, hoping that Spot would appear. When the two weeks' stray hold was up, Spot's photo was finally posted. However, instead of saying Spot was available for adoption, they said she had been dropped off *that same day* with parvo (a highly contagious gastrointestinal virus that can be prevented with a vaccine but otherwise can lead to death if untreated) and were asking for money.

I was furious. Unable to keep my mouth shut, I called them out on their social media post (I assure you this is not usually like me). I explained that Spot was surrendered healthy two weeks prior and must have caught parvo in their kennel facility. They were lying about the circumstances and exploiting Spot for money they would most likely pocket. This groomer and rescue was a fully staffed business, with lots of money behind it and an A-list following. In response, their social media person covered up the truth I was trying to share and blocked me within a few hours. I got tons of DMs from strangers who had also experienced or heard bad things about this rescue, but there was nothing more I could do. It became apparent I wasn't the only person who had tried to take them down. In fact, I learned that legal professionals had unsuccessfully tried to close them down before.

Months after this incident, I received another DM, this one with screenshots of a text conversation between the groomer and the rescue employees about Spot. The conversation revealed that Spot had passed away because she was never given the medical treatment she needed while on stray hold. The last text sent demanded that nobody was to give adoption information over the phone, and that if anyone asked what happened to Spot, they were to say she was adopted by someone on their committee. The reason I tell you this sad story is to show that not all organizations calling themselves rescues are good. There are a lot of people in it for the money and a pat on the back. People love to be told they're a hero, but a true hero is one that's selfless and in it for the right reasons. A true hero is in it for the dog.

Questions to Consider When Choosing a Rescue

(Hint, hint: the answers to these questions should be yes.)

- ◯ Do all their social media, PayPal, and Venmo accounts match?

- ◯ Are they a registered nonprofit or 501(c)(3) charity?

- ◯ Are they transparent with their audience? (That is, do they write honest and detailed descriptions of their dogs, or is it all rainbows and unicorns?)

- ◯ Are they willing to share where the dog came from and the story behind getting it?

- ◯ Are they willing to help you find the perfect dog?

- ◯ Are they willing to work with you after you've adopted a dog from them to ensure it will be a successful adoption?

○ Do they send their dogs home with microchips?

○ Do they provide you with medical records?

○ Are they adamant about spaying and neutering? If the dog is old enough, does he or she come fixed?

○ Do they have an adoption fee? (Free dogs are a red flag. Rescues need adoption fees in order to properly care for each dog they take in. Having no adoption fee is unrealistic.)

○ Does their website provide ample information about their rescue?

○ Do they have a policy that says you cannot give this dog away to anyone without their approval?

Thanks to the power of social media, I not only found out the truth about Spot and that rescue but I also discovered the most amazing *legitimate* rescue, Mutt Scouts, an organization founded by Nikki Audet that's stationed in both San Diego and Los Angeles. I really connected with Mutt Scouts. Since fostering is solely volunteer work, feeling a connection with a rescue organization and ensuring you share the same values are incredibly important. Mutt Scouts instantly made me feel at home. When I applied, I quickly heard back from a foster coordinator named Amelie who did my home check, informed me about how the rescue was run, and communicated regularly with me once I began fostering.

Q&A with Nikki Audet, Founder of Mutt Scouts

VICTORIA SHAFFER: When did you first become interested in dog rescue?

NIKKI AUDET: I became interested in dog rescue when I moved to Los Angeles from New England. I'd never seen stray dogs before then. I started volunteering at the South LA shelter taking photos of dogs for adoption to post on the internet. It was at the beginning of when shelter animals were being networked online. The more I would go, the more I would get attached. But then the next time I'd come in, those dogs had all been euthanized. So,

I started just pulling [rescuing] the dogs I'd see being brought back to be euthanized.

V: A lot of people are passionate about dog rescue, but not many have the courage to start their very own rescue—what inspired you to go big?

N: Since I started rescue, I knew it was what I was supposed to do. I knew I would never stop doing it, so really, it's just commitment. I've seen a lot of rescues come and go, but I just keep going. We have the best team ever now, so I know world domination is next.

V: Do you have a favorite rescue story?

N: There are so many! I've been doing this for, like, eighteen years, so it's hard to pick. Running your own rescue takes complete dedication. What keeps you going, and what helps keep the rescue running? So much time, money, and resilience are needed. It took a lot of sacrifice over the years. I do this full-time and don't get paid, so it's kinda the dumbest and best thing ever. I have a husband who's an artist, so we're both happy with empty pockets and full hearts. We've been homeless several times, no money in the bank, and so forth, but that's just the way it goes.

V: Mutt Scouts is known for taking in a lot of special-needs and medical dogs that most other rescues would turn away. Knowing how expensive it can be and how difficult it is to find homes for these dogs, why do you still take them in?

N: Because that's what rescues are supposed to do! Take the dogs that need help the most. I've always been passionate about underdogs. I've always looked for what shelters need the most help—what dogs are getting euthanized. I like street rescue because a lot of times we're their only hope.

V: Mutt Scouts rescues a lot of Mexican street dogs. How did you get connected with the rescuers in Tijuana finding dogs every day?

N: Once I moved to San Diego, I followed some Mexican animal rescue pages and started working with a few Mexican rescuers. The word got out that not only would we take a lot of REALLY hard cases but we'd also always update the original rescuers on where the dogs went. So, they saw the great happy ending for these dogs that had had, for example, their faces ripped off. We suddenly had many, many people writing about dogs they'd found in terrible situations, wanting us to help.

V: What would you say to those who need to be convinced to adopt a dog rather than buy one?

N: Open your eyes and look around you at the animals suffering in the world. Get your head out of your ass and do something good for another soul that needs it.

V: There are so many dogs in need. How do you decide which dogs to take into Mutt Scouts?

N: I think we take a lot more dogs than we should most of the time. We just make it work!

V: What's the difference between a rescue organization and an animal shelter run by the county or city?

N: Rescues can pick what animals they take; city shelters have open admission and have to take all dogs and animals in their precinct. That's one reason why I think all rescues should take on some harder-to-adopt dogs—seniors, power breeds, the sick, and the injured—to take some of the burden off city shelters. Rescues that only select highly adoptable animals, in my opinion, suck. That's not rescue. You gotta always have some seniors, definitely some pits, some Chihuahuas—the types of dogs that are overcrowding the shelters—or you suck as a rescue.

V: What advice do you have for people who want to start fostering?

N: Oh gosh, fostering is one of my favorite things about being a rescuer— helping an animal in need, helping them come out of their shell, letting them feel safe and loved. I can't really describe how rewarding it is.

V: What's the best way that people can help if they can't rescue a dog?

N: There are so many ways—think about what you're good at, then make it into something to help rescue organizations. Are you good at writing? Help write dog descriptions, apply for grants, and help with social media. Are you a good photographer? Take pics for the website / social media to help dogs get adopted. You love being active? Volunteer to walk dogs!

My first foster through Mutt Scouts was a pug named Louis. Amelie prepared me to take in Louis, filling me in on everything she knew about him physically, emotionally, and behaviorally. She coordinated his drop-off at my home and made sure he was sent with all his necessities—food, leash, collar with Mutt Scouts tag, harness, and even a few belly bands (male diapers—

Louis had a bad habit of marking inside the home). After just a few days of having Louis, Amelie had already found him the perfect family. She connected me with this family to schedule a meet and greet, during which, if the family thought it was a match, they would be able to take Louis home right then and there.

It was the most seamless fostering experience I'd ever had, and because of that, I was motivated to do it again. Amelie was organized and motivated to get my foster dogs adopted in a timely manner. Amelie was like the really good agent nobody ever

Louis

had. She listened to me and trusted my instincts, which gave me the confidence to take on harder fosters like the Pup Stars, a litter of nine puppies and their unsocialized and timid mama (you'll learn about them in the next chapter).

> "Navigating early adulthood in a big city like San Diego after growing up in small-town Ohio was nothing short of a learning curve. Even with hundreds of thousands of more people than I have ever known, I spent most days feeling lonely and like I didn't have a purpose. It wasn't until I joined Mutt Scouts' team that I truly felt at home here. It goes without saying that being a part of Mutt Scouts' mission has done more for me than I have ever done for it."
>
> —KAILEE BROWN,
> kennel volunteer at Mutt Scouts

As I grew into a larger role with Mutt Scouts, Amelie introduced me to the other dedicated coordinators—Brooke and Shayna—and to the incredible founder, Nikki. The team included me in daily conversations and valued my opinions. Whenever I had an idea—whether about fundraising, content, or otherwise—they humored me. I feel so fortunate to be a Mutt Scouts coordinator myself now among a team of passionate, genuine women who put dogs first and themselves second. I found my people. These girls are badass, and they'd take a bullet for our dogs.

SAM AND SHAYNA LESSER

February 3, 2019, was the first day I officially volunteered for Mutt Scouts. Since that day, my life has grown in the most amazing (sometimes sad, frustrating, and annoying, but always rewarding) way.

I had been following Mutt Scouts on social media along with a handful of other local rescues since I moved to LA a few years prior. I was most drawn to Mutt Scouts because of the extreme medical cases they took in. Watching Mutts Scouts take these dogs that'd been injured, abused, and forgotten, then giving them the love, care, and attention they needed broke my heart and filled me with hope. I teared up anytime I would watch one of their stories and knew I wanted to help in any way I could.

I had wanted to volunteer with Mutt Scouts for a while, but the timing never worked out with my schedule. And frankly, as much as I wanted to volunteer, I was intimidated. I didn't know how I could help or what I could do. Finally, the day before the Super Bowl in 2019, they posted that they needed a volunteer to do transport the next day. This was the perfect opportunity. Here was something I could do, and seeing as I had no interest in watching football, I sent them a message offering to help. To my surprise, they got back to me immediately and coordinated for me to pick up some dogs from an adoption event in San Diego to bring them to their foster homes in Los Angeles.

I picked up three dogs—a boxer mix named Maeve and two medium-size mutts named Woody and Wolfie. My job was to transport them. Simple enough. But something happened when I met Wolfie, and I was pretty sure I'd have to change course. I reached out to the director and asked if there was any way I could bring Wolfie home to foster (and potentially adopt).

My husband and I had been thinking about getting another dog for a while, but we weren't actively looking. We have another rescue named Rodney, who was eight at the time and was very picky with dogs (and humans, and inanimate objects—you get it). We couldn't decide whether getting another dog would bring a little bit of joy and excitement to his life or ruin it. Luckily, I was told I could bring Wolfie home to foster, so we could find out. That was the beginning of what I'm sure will be a lifetime in rescue.

Now, almost two years later, Wolfie, now Sam, is curled up beside me on the couch, his front paw on my arm as I type and Rodney right next to him. I wouldn't say he and Rodney are best friends, but they are brothers who have each other's backs.

Volunteering that day has changed my life in more ways than I ever could have imagined. I volunteered to transport, which turned into fostering, which turned into adopting, which allowed me to meet the amazing women who run Mutt Scouts. I slowly became more and more in-

Rodney and Sam

volved, and now I'm one of six women who help run the rescue. We put our blood, sweat, and tears into our dogs and work every single day to make sure they have anything they need, from foster homes to surgeries to good ol' TLC. There's nothing more rewarding than seeing a dog who was once neglected and living on the street go to a home where they're loved. I'm so grateful that I get to see these transformations up close and personal and be a tiny part of their rescue journeys.

I *hate* football, but Super Bowl Sunday will forever be a day I celebrate because it's one of the days that truly changed my life. Not only did I get the most amazing dog in the world, but it led me to working with Mutt Scouts and acquiring this family of incredible dog-loving women.

— Shayna Lerner,

foster coordinator at Mutt Scouts

As I mentioned before, I truly appreciate how open and collaborative Mutt Scouts is. In the early days of my time with Mutt Scouts, when I was fostering the Pup Stars litter at the beginning of the coronavirus pandemic, they let me run with a fundraising idea I called "Concert for a Cause." I put together a lineup of musicians, actors, and comedians to help raise money over Instagram Live. I have all these wonderful, talented connections—why not use them to help these pups? Katie Kimmel, an artist, dog lover, and friend of Mutt Scouts, created exclusive Mutt Scouts T-shirts for the Instagram event, and they sold like hotcakes. We raised around $20,000 for Mutt Scouts and then spent it on medical bills, trainers, and supplies in no time, like any fully functioning rescue must.

Streaming on Instagram Live with (clockwise from top left):

Tove Lo

Dad (Paul Shaffer)

Gilbert Gottfriend

Katie Kimmel

Abby Elliott

For those who might not know, a rescue organization is expected to provide all medical care and necessary supplies at no cost to their foster volunteers. That's expensive! At the very minimum, this includes a routine vet visit, food, an appropriately sized crate or pen, toys, a bed or blanket, a leash, a harness, and a collar with a rescue contact tag. Luckily, many of these supplies can be reused again and again with each new foster dog, but food and medical bills add up quickly. Speaking from experience, a large litter of puppies, plus their mom who has to eat five times a day to produce enough milk for her puppies, can go through nearly two bags of kibble a week. This doesn't include the costly formula, supplements, preventive medication, and canned food that's bought on top of that. Once you add vaccinating and microchipping, medical bills for ill dogs, and training and rehab bills for abused dogs, the money goes fast.

Money-Saving Tips for Fostering Litters

While fostering is free to do, as all supplies are covered by the rescue service (or at least should be, but let's be real—everyone spends extra money spoiling their fosters), raising puppies is a massive expense for those who rescue, and adoption fees don't even make a dent in covering that expense. Here are tips I've picked up along the way to save money when helping dogs in need:

DESIGNATE A SOILED-LINEN AREA. (I use a large trash can with a lid that I keep in my backyard.) Wash linens on hot with unscented, paraben-free laundry detergent that you can buy in bulk. You'll be doing laundry regularly. HANG DRY your puppy laundry to save on energy bills.

MAKE CLEANING SPRAY out of white vinegar and water using a one-to-three ratio.

USE PLASTIC POOP BAGS TO CLEAN UP POOP BEFORE WASHING LINENS. These "poop bags" can be shopping bags, produce bags, or even plastic wrapping from any goods. (I keep a trash can for poop bags next to my soiled-linen trash can.)

MAKE YOUR OWN PEE PADS. You can use recycled cardboard, newspaper, and paper bags.

USE RAGS OR CUT-UP OLD TOWELS TO CLEAN UP MESSES instead of spending money on paper towels. These can go in your soiled-linen can.

GIVE YOUR FOSTER COORDINATOR PLENTY OF NOTICE IF YOU'RE RUNNING OUT OF NECESSITIES like kibble and wee wee pads so they can find a good deal and order them for you in a timely manner.

NEVER ORDER SUPPLIES FOR YOUR LITTER WITHOUT YOUR RESCUE'S APPROVAL unless you plan to pay for it yourself.

MAKE YOUR OWN TOYS! Braiding ripped towels and sheets make for perfect puppy tug toys. (See page 27.)

Besides having all the necessary supplies and more, it's important to keep a schedule when fostering. As my résumé of fosters expands, so does my caretaking knowledge. I can predict bathroom habits, spot safety hazards, and set up accordingly the minute I meet a dog or puppy based on their age and temperament. If you plan to foster, you might eventually learn this skill, too.

Whenever people ask how I'm able to raise puppies and care for so many dogs at once, I tell them that it's all in keeping with a schedule. My morning routine, for example, is as follows: At 7 a.m., I wake the dogs up and move them outside. Having two playpens for the puppies (one inside and one outside) and a fenced-in yard for the independent dogs allows me to rid the inside of my house of everyone so I can clean up the mess they made overnight. No matter how many puppies eight weeks and under I've fostered, the amount of mess these tiny creatures manage to make in a single night still shocks me every morning. Without disgusting you with too much detail, all I'll say is thank goodness for the ability to breathe through your mouth and for the powerful water pressure of a hose.

Anyway, once the puppy nursery is clean, I prepare everyone's food. It's a long process to feed so many dogs. I'm usually so hungry by this point in my morning and dreaming about an unhealthy bagel with cream cheese, but I must make sure everyone is taken care of first. I am a Hebrew school dropout. I never really enjoyed going. But the one thing that stuck with me was that the Torah says a person must always feed their animals before themselves. Echo and Rue are perfect, patient foster siblings, waiting for me to feed all our guests before them. Then after Echo and Rue are fed, you better believe that bagel is being popped into the toaster immediately.

For the puppy food, I have a designated blender used specifically for this purpose. In it, I blend kibble I've soaked overnight (in order to soften it), canned wet food, powdered milk replacer formula, and some nutritional Dyne for an extra boost with warm water. It's like a protein smoothie for puppies! Then I pour the mixture into a baking sheet or cupcake tin. It looks as though I'm baking a delicious cake, but trust me—that potent smell is nothing close to sweet batter. In puppy-raising terms, this is called gruel. Gruel is typically served to puppies starting around three to four weeks of age. It's thicker than milk but softer than mush. Gruel, which is made from

the same kibble they'll eventually be eating dry, is used to wean puppies off their mom's milk.

Introducing puppies to solid foods is a long process. The transition from milk to kibble takes several weeks (that's right—I make this blended bad boy for the puppies for *several weeks*).

As the puppies get older and their teeth come in, I gradually thicken the mixture by decreasing the water, subtracting first the formula, then Dyne, then the canned wet food, until they're eating kibble moistened with a bit of water. To better explain the consistency, I often compare it to human food: start with the consistency of formula, gradually thicken it to a pureed soup, then chunky oatmeal. By seven weeks I can (finally) forget the blender and combine just the soaked kibble with a bit of canned wet food until eventually, by eight weeks (when the puppies are old enough to be separated from their mother), they're eating as a typical dog would.

Did I mention that *everything* to do with puppies is messy? Even them learning how to eat is a messy process. They walk through their food, stick their noses in it, and track it all over the floor *and* their siblings. It's utter chaos. Not even Jackson Pollock could come close.

I also deworm the puppies before they're adopted, which only adds to the mess. I could do without finding the white, chalky dewormer all over my arms, legs, and in my hair even after a shower, but of course, that'd be asking for too much. With a warm washcloth, I have to wipe down each puppy, paying special attention to their paws and face. Then, one by one, I move each puppy into the indoor pen where they can cuddle up next to Mama to stay warm. In the case of the Charcuterie litter where Mama was absent, I placed the puppies on top of heating pads on a low-medium setting (so as not to burn them) that I hid under a cozy blanket. They looked so precious, all cozy and warm and cuddled up together with bloated, full bellies—the perfect cocktail for a long nap until their next feeding. This routine happens again and again throughout the day, depending on the age and stage of feeding they're in. Finally, before bed, when the puppies are nice and tired, I weigh each one to ensure they're getting enough food and growing accordingly.

As I hope you can now see, it's a lot of work—hours spent cleaning, feeding, and tending to whining puppies—but it's a job I'm more than happy to do. Even when the dogs are satiated and sleeping, and the house is finally peaceful, I find myself scrolling through photos and videos of the puppies on my phone until they wake up again. When I'm in between litters, I think, *What am I supposed to do with all this free time?* Puppy raising fills me with so much joy and, let's be honest, stunts me from having children in my twenties. I'm addicted to it.

People often ask how I'm able to "give away" foster puppies after raising them. They insist they could never foster because they'd get too attached. What I always say in response is that *of course* it's difficult saying goodbye to puppies you've watched grow, puppies you've worked for and worried about around the clock. But knowing that he or she is going to a great family for a wonderful life makes it that much easier. Plus, let's be real—one feels a bit of a relief when the work's over, no matter how briefly.

I love receiving updates, photos, and videos from the new owners. It further ingrains my opinion that, as a dog foster, you play a pivotal role in this dog's and this family's story and happiness. If you're choosing to not foster because you think it'll be too hard on you emotionally, I say this: Put your emotions aside and help a dog in need. The positives will always outweigh the negatives.

Six

COVID-K9

---- 🐾 ----

FOCUSING ON
THE GOOD DURING
THE BAD

My first COVID-19 pandemic fosters were Madonna and her nine puppies—

Britney Spears, Justin Bieber, Ricky Martin, Selena, Lady Gaga, P!nk, Harry Styles, Shawn Mendes, and Ariana Grande. I referred to them as the "Pup Stars." Madonna was a timid dog and an escape artist who had little to no interest in human interaction, but she was the best mom I've ever witnessed. She was incredibly attentive to her puppies, always by their side. The Pup Stars never went hungry, because Madonna was right there whenever they needed her. Mutt Scouts rescued Madonna from a high-kill shelter where she was scheduled to be euthanized with all the puppies still in her womb.

Safe in her new foster home, Madonna delivered the nine Pup Stars under the watchful eye of her foster, Riley, a badass twenty-three-year-old, who became a dear friend of mine. Rescue work not only saves lives, but also brings like-minded people together like Riley and me.

MADONNA AND RILEY O'DAY

The night I got Madonna inside my apartment and opened her crate, it was evident that she had never been in a home before. She ducked back inside in complete terror the moment she noticed the ceiling above her head. Trying to comfort her was not helpful because, for Madonna, people were not

a soothing entity. She wanted nothing to do with me, and I could not get closer than five feet without her shrinking into the corner to make herself as small as possible. If my heart hadn't completely broken from seeing her photo at the shelter, then watching her wince and try to disappear out of my sight in the corner finished the job.

Before I brought Madonna home, the shelter labeled her as a "fear-biter" and consequently put her on the euthanasia list. Mutt

5   "Pet Statistics," ASPCA, https://www.aspca.org/animal-homelessness/shelter-intake-and-surrender/pet-statistics.

Scouts pulled her from the shelter just in time. Underweight, pregnant, scooped off the streets, and tossed into a cage at the shelter, it's clear why she felt afraid and vulnerable. She tried to bite at the shelter not because she was aggressive, but because she was stressed out and scared.

Her bony, emaciated body stood in stark contrast to the blimp that was her pregnant belly. She was visibly filthy; embedded in her fur hid a nasty flea infestation and fat, freshly fed ticks. She was so fearful that a bath before she gave birth was not in the cards for her. With help from friends, I managed to get her in the car to go to the vet the next afternoon. The X-ray revealed that she was carrying not six, not eight, but *ten* puppies.

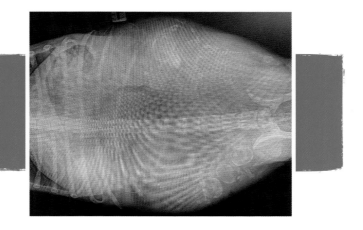

I got her settled back home, ordered a same-day-delivery baby pool to function as her whelping box, and headed off to the pet store to pick up supplies. When I arrived back home less than a half hour later, I heard loud squeals from the bedroom where she was staying. I opened the door, and sure enough, a Beanie Baby–size black puppy was wriggling around on the dog bed I had set up for her on my bathroom floor. Upon seeing me enter, Madonna abruptly got up and hid in the corner. I dried the puppy off and moved it into the towel-lined crate, where to my relief Madonna followed and began to nurse him.

Riley

The next fourteen hours were full of highs and lows. Madonna became less focused on her fear toward me and more focused on delivering her puppies. The first six puppies were a breeze, but she became exhausted as we approached hour ten. She needed to rest and regain some strength, so I dimmed the lights and gave her some space. What happened next shattered me—Madonna gave birth to a stillborn. I knew something was wrong when I walked in to check on her, and the puppy, about half the size of his littermates, was still and deliberately placed several feet away from the rest. It was apparent that Madonna had cleaned him up and knew he was gone.

I immediately FaceTimed Mutt Scouts founder and puppy-birthing expert Nikki, who walked me through giving the puppy CPR. I tried for thirty painful minutes to revive the puppy, gave him mouth-to-mouth resuscitation with chest compressions, and I tried my best to clear every last bit of amniotic fluid from his nose and mouth. After a half hour of desperate attempts, his gums remained colorless, and I saw no signs of life. I was devastated, but Madonna still had three more puppies to birth, and I had to focus on making sure they made it safely Earth-side.

The next two puppies were stuck in the canal and wouldn't budge for several minutes. With help over FaceTime from Nikki, I assisted them out of the canal. Gloves were not an option, because they were impossible to find in stock during the first surge of the COVID-19 pandemic, so this was a job where I quite literally had to get my hands dirty.

While the first stuck puppy came out with no complications, the second was not as simple. The second puppy would not breathe, and every second felt like minutes. I was terrified to lose another puppy, and after a minute or so of letting Madonna try to stimulate the puppy's breathing on her own, I began CPR. Eventually, the puppy let out a loud cry. It felt like a scene from a movie. I breathed a gigantic sigh of relief, placed the puppy back with Madonna to nurse, and almost immediately delivered the final, healthy puppy with my adrenaline high.

Nine healthy puppies nursed from their mom, who could finally relax and put her head down. I was so thankful to have Nikki and the Mutt Scouts team available and ready to walk me through every step of the process to ensure that the delivery was as successful as possible. I can say with 100 percent certainty that delivering and foster-

ing Madonna's puppies was an unforgettably incredible experience. Although the loss of one puppy crushed me, I had to remind myself that we saved nine healthy puppies and their mom who otherwise never would have had a chance. They are ten future best friends for ten lucky families.

— *Riley O'Day,*

Mutt Scouts foster

When the Pup Star puppies turned one month old, Riley handed them over to me to finish raising them. During this time, California was abiding by a stay-at-home order, so there was really nothing else to do besides play with and stare at these adorable, tiny puppies. My oldest friend Maysie (remember her from chapter 1?) locked down with me at my home, and together we raised these pop star puppies with love and devotion.

From the very start, Maysie and I looked forward to weighing these puppies each day. When evening finally came, Maysie and I were exhausted, sweaty, and covered in puppy gruel (among other less pleasant things), but no matter how tired we were, we'd race to take out a mixing bowl, place it on top of a kitchen scale, and weigh all nine puppies one by one. We asked each other, "Do you think Justin Bieber's going to reach six pounds today?" or "Will Britney Spears stay the smallest forever?" It became our little ritual. Typically, Maysie read the scale and I recorded their daily weight on a color-coded chart. Giddy with excitement (or delusional from exhaustion), we sang each puppy a song by the artist they were named after, FaceTiming friends to join in on the silly fun. I question if it would've been as thrilling had we not all been stuck at home with nowhere to go and nothing to do, but we ran with it. Why question happiness?

The puppy weigh-ins somehow evolved into nightly Instagram Live shows I hosted on my page. The audience grew from just friends and family to dog lovers all across the country, and it happened pretty quickly. During the uncertain time of COVID-19, our little Instagram Live weigh-in became a community of respite. Everyone greeted each other in the comments, shared stories about dogs they had at home, and even bet on how much each puppy would weigh that evening. Though we were all locked in our homes, unable to physically meet, it felt like Maysie and I had an army of puppy lovers there with us during each weigh-in, rooting them (and us) on. It felt like we really knew them.

Because of this love, there was a comfort level that allowed me to be myself—goofy, creative, and often in my pajamas picking on Maysie. I nicknamed Maysie "Vanna White" because she was the ultimate puppy weigh-in assistant. We created segments out of thin air, like when we celebrated a puppy growing from one pound to two. We called it joining the prestigious "two-pound club," and everyone cheered in the comments as Maysie held up the puppy to do a little celebratory dance. Each weigh-in concluded with a roundup, which always began with me shouting, "R-R-R-ROUNDUPPPP!" as if I were an announcer at a sporting event. I named off the puppies from smallest to largest as Maysie held them up like Rafiki holding up Simba in *The Lion King*. It was wacky but so very special at the same time. That nightly live stream is what got many of us through lockdown.

Because of the puppy weigh-ins and the surprising number of dogs quarantining in my home, several morning shows suddenly wanted to feature us. It turns out that our story was a breath of fresh air during an otherwise depressing and confusing time. I accepted the offers to come on the air and tell my story in hopes of spreading the word about the importance of rescue and adoption (the same reason I wrote this book).

During the *Tamron Hall Show* pre-interview, one of the writers asked my permission to title the segment "How Fostering Saved My Life." Even for daytime television, I thought this was a bit extreme. I was hesitant to agree to it, thinking viewers might conclude I was being overdramatic. But the producers were insistent, feeling strongly about the segment's positive and life-altering message.

After some debate, I agreed. I started to realize that with the coronavirus spreading as rapidly as it was, perhaps fostering really *did* save my life. When COVID first hit, I'd already committed to fostering Madonna and her puppies. Though it was scary to be across the country from my family while grocery store shelves began to empty and panic ensued, I was firm in my decision to stay in California and care for Echo, Rue, and my ten fosters. They needed me; it was the right thing to do.

My family is spread around the East Coast in New York, Florida, and Maryland. Across all three states, my parents and relatives caught the virus. First, my aunt in Miami was put into a twelve-day medicated coma; then my dad contracted the virus, followed by my mom being hospitalized with it. As soon as we thought we were out of the woods, my aunt and uncle in Maryland went to the hospital with the virus, too. Two of my best friends, Gabby and Rachel, also came down with coronavirus. To say that I was concerned would be an understatement. The unknowns made it all very scary.

I was the only person in my social circle in Los Angeles who was related to and knew people affected by COVID-19 this early on. People were telling me I had bad luck. It was the most frightening thing I've ever had to go through. Not having answers, struggling to secure my mom a bed in the hospital initially, afraid to call in the morning not knowing if everyone had made it through the night—I don't wish that uncertainty and fear upon anyone.

But throughout that uncertainty and fear, the puppies helped the days go by, and my new Instagram community provided support. Had I not been preoccupied with my fosters in Los Angeles, I would've fled home to New York as soon as my dad fell ill since we didn't know what it was at the time. If that had been the case, there's no doubt in my mind that I, too, would have contracted the virus. Who knows where I'd be now?

Beyond the risk of catching COVID-19, everyone around me felt incredibly down as they adjusted to this new world. Jobs were cut, social gatherings were cancelled, and once-busy streets became abandoned. Yet somehow, despite all of this, I managed to create a little bubble for myself, and in that bubble were Maysie, Echo, Rue, Mama Madonna, and nine puppies. Everything I needed, except maybe a boyfriend.

The stay-at-home order fostered creativity in me and also turned Maysie into an excellent cook. While Maysie was whipping up delicious meals in the kitchen, I created an Instagram TV series called *COVID-K9*. Every week I taught doggy DIY projects to keep your dog entertained, using household items in the comfort and safety of your own home. Once I let go of the pressure of perfection and gave Maysie's arm a break after insisting she hold the camera so still, I had so much fun doing those projects and watching others try them, too. Between the Instagram Live streams and *COVID-K9* series, Madonna's Pup Star litter had become my muse. Thanks to them, I can look back at quarantine and focus on the good instead of the bad.

Seven

COMMITMENT ISSUES

KNOWING WHEN THE TIME IS RIGHT

I've spoken to many people in my generation who grew up with dogs

yet haven't—for one reason or another—committed to getting one in their adult life. That, obviously, is the opposite of me: I adopted two dogs at nineteen, and a third at twenty-seven. Remember how Maysie and her family inspired my passion and love for dogs? This chapter is where her dog story comes full circle.

You should know Maysie and I are kind of an odd duo. We're yin and yang. Maysie is the athletic one; I'm the creative one. Maysie is the shy one; I'm the one who never shuts up. Maysie hates makeup and fashion, but I love 'em. She's laid-back, and I'm anxiety ridden. Maysie also just reminded me that she's very tall and I'm very short, so thanks for that, Maysie.

However, despite all these differences, there's one important thing we have in common: we both absolutely love and adore dogs. Our families spend Christmas together, and Maysie and I always save watching that year's big dog movie until Christmas Day. One Christmas we watched *The Art of Racing in the Rain*, and the year before that we watched *A Dog's Purpose*. Without fail, Maysie always cries throughout the entirety of each movie, and we all laugh at the

wet tissues scattered around her. Christmas is the one time a year I see Maysie show any emotion (she's going to kill me for saying that).

My secret plan for Maysie was coming into fruition when she agreed to raise the Pup Star litter in quarantine with me. You see, I always hoped she'd adopt one of my foster puppies. I knew she would be the best dog mom—I'd seen it before when we were kids. She just needed a little push and a little confidence to become one again as an adult. Growing up, Maysie and I had tons of sleepovers where we spent evenings scrolling through Petfinder, imagining what it would be like if one of us adopted any particular dog we saw. We'd hypothetically rename each dog we liked based on the vibes their pictures gave off. Maysie always said she was going to name her first dog Edith—Edie for short. There was something about old-fashioned names for a dog that we thought was hysterical—Ethyl, Gladys, Eunice, Harold, Melvin . . . true doggy-name gems. But when the time finally came to rename the pup Maysie eventually adopted, she decided to go with a more modern name, because that pup gave off her own special vibe.

She wavered for a long time about adopting a dog. She put a lot of pressure on the idea of being the perfect dog mom when, really, there's no such thing. It's a big commitment to get a puppy—financially, especially—but I knew she'd be great. She finally decided she would adopt a pup from the Pup Star litter, but then she encountered another bump in the road. Which would she pick? As potential adopters visited the puppies, Maysie was overwhelmed with the decision to choose just one. She truly loved them all. One night, I captured a video of Maysie watching them all sleep and tearing up as she thought about the day they were going to get adopted and leave us. It was like her watching a dog movie on Christmas Day all over again.

When our second pair of adopters came with the intention of adopting Shawn Mendes, I knew it was going to be a rough one for Maysie. Shawn was the model puppy of the litter; he also happened to be one of Maysie's favorites. While she considered choosing Shawn, Maysie ultimately decided that if the couple coming to meet him really wanted him, she'd let them have him. "They're really nice. He'll have a good life," she made out through all the tears. In the end, Maysie adopted Britney Spears, the runt of the Pup Star litter. "I'm going to name her Piper—Pipes for short," she announced decidedly. Choosing Piper hadn't come easily to Maysie, but I know Maysie is happy with her choice now. I asked her some questions about her latest adoption journey:

Q&A with Maysie Makrianes

VICTORIA SHAFFER: What did you think about me adopting two dogs when we were nineteen?

MAYSIE MAKRIANES: I couldn't imagine myself getting two puppies our first year of college. I thought it was a little nuts, but I couldn't wait to visit. I knew you'd be a great dog mom. I remember my mother was surprisingly all for it and told your mom to let you do it.

V: This is why I love your mom! So, growing up with so many dogs, how come you didn't get your own dog sooner?

M: I'm a homebody, so I always went home a lot during college and continued to have a strong bond with my family's dogs. I had a typical college experience that differed from yours, so it wasn't an option to get a dog that early. After college, I traveled a bit, so I knew I wanted to be at a stable point before bringing a new dog into my life.

V: When did you know you were ready to get your first adult-life dog?

M: After living in Los Angeles for a year and a half, I felt like I had a great support system here. I intend on living in LA for the long run, and it's a great city to have a dog in. I finally felt like I was financially ready and that I was able to give the time, effort, and love it takes to raise a pup. I'd done most of the things I wanted to do and, in my late twenties, no longer had "FOMO." Haha!

V: Maysie with the hip lingo. How and why did you finally choose Piper, formerly Britney Spears?

M: As you know, it was a tough decision. Once I decided to adopt a dog from the litter, I spent a great deal of time falling in love with each and every puppy for their own unique personalities and characteristics. I tried to picture each one in my life. Piper was always climbing into my lap and sleeping in my sweatshirt pocket. When we'd wake up everyone each morning, the other puppies would rush outside, but Piper would still be fast asleep. You *know* how much I love sleep. I saw a little bit of myself in her, and I just loved her cute little face. When I finally chose, it just felt right. Every dog owner knows the feeling when they choose or meet their dog and it just feels right.

V: I am still waiting for that feeling with a man. What changes did you have to make in your life in order to adopt Piper?

M: At the time, I was living in a building that wasn't dog friendly. The first thing I had to do before getting approved to adopt Piper was to move. I found a one-bedroom apartment a block away from the beach where I knew Piper and I would enjoy taking our daily walks. I also had to change my shift at work and find a doggy day care with similar hours to mine nearby. As opposed to working early mornings, I now wake up with Piper, take her on a walk, eat breakfast, run errands, and then drop her off at day care on my way to work. It's like having a kid. Before Piper, I was never a routine person, and now one of the most important things that keep Piper and me going is a schedule. Piper has helped me become a proper adult, and I know that you and my mom are thankful for that.

V: Amen to that. Maysie is finally adulting! So, what advice do you have for anyone looking to get their first dog?

M: This puppy is going to rely on you for everything. You'll be responsible for guiding this dog through the world, and everything you do will affect their life. There will be challenging times, but everything you and your dog go through together will be absolutely worth it. In no time, you won't be able to imagine life without your dog.

Piper in her new collar and tag

The day Maysie made the decision to adopt Piper, I was ecstatic. My longest and dearest friend—the person who introduced me to dogs in the first place—was getting a dog because of me! I was so excited to welcome Piper into our family (I demanded to be her aunt and godmother) that I rushed Maysie out of the house to go shopping at the pet supply store—my favorite part of welcoming a new puppy. In particular, I love picking out the perfect collar and leash to complement their coat, and I love seeing the puppy's name engraved on a tag for the first time.

Maysie and I often reminisce about how small and adorable Piper was. Piper has grown into a thirty-five-pound beautiful and playful dog who, when reunited with her former foster siblings, Echo and Rue, and her best friend, Alfie, can't stop kissing them and yipping with joy. I can't imagine Maysie without Piper anymore. She's a part of our family; she even got her first stocking this Christmas.

If you love dogs but you're worried about whether or not you're ready to have one of your own, check in with yourself to see what's really giving you pause. Dogs are a big responsibility, so checking to see if you have the finances as well as the time to dedicate to them is a must. But remember: there's no such thing as a perfect dog parent. You won't always be perfect, and it won't always be easy, but if it's something you truly want, explore what's needed to help make adopting a dog your reality. Remember to always take into consideration the following questions when determining whether or not you're ready to take the plunge.

Important Questions to Ask Yourself Before Adopting a Dog

1. If you have other pets, how will they react to a new family member?

2. Is your current home suitable for the dog you want? That is, is your yard securely fenced? Do you have wall-to-wall carpeting that needs to be protected? Are all hazardous items put away / out of reach? Is there enough space for you and your dog to coexist comfortably?

3. How will you incorporate your new dog into your schedule?

4. Is everyone in the household on board with adding a dog to the family? Does anyone have allergies or an aversion to the mess and hair that come along with having a dog?

5. What do you want to do with your dog? Do you want an active dog to go hiking or running with or one to cuddle on the couch with?

6. Do you plan to travel with your dog? If not, who will care for your dog while you are away? If yes, how big is too big to travel with?

7. If you're thinking about getting a puppy, are you ready for the time commitment and patience you will need to train him or her?

8. Are you prepared to be financially responsible for your dog? Think supplies, food, routine care, and even health emergencies . . .

9. Are you committed to this dog if he or she grows bigger than expected, develops behavioral issues, or has unexpected health problems?

Eight

FUR REAL

--- 🐾 ---

THE IMPORTANCE OF RESCUE EDUCATION

Lily and her six newborn puppies were found in a cardboard box on the side of the freeway

by a family who contacted Mutt Scouts for guidance. Thankfully, Mutt Scouts was able to convince them to surrender the dogs, as the puppies were fragile and needed to be cared for by someone with experience. That's where I came in. I was given the family's address and went as soon as I could with my friend to pick up the dogs. Let me tell you, rescuing comes with its own obstacles, but rescuing during a pandemic is in an entirely different league. I would take all the help I could get.

Since we weren't allowed to enter the home, we waited outside with our masks and hand sanitizers for Lily and her puppies to be brought out. After about thirty minutes, the gate finally opened and out came Lily, except she was running for the freeway. A woman came sprinting out behind her, chasing her with a towel and screaming her name. My friend and I looked at each other, frozen in fear. All we could do was wait in the hopes that the woman would be able to get a hold of Lily and bring her back to us. The woman eventually returned, dragging a wheezing Lily with a towel wrapped around her neck as some kind of crude, makeshift lead. How had she been caring for Lily for an entire week without a proper collar and leash? Lily choking was a sight I had to unsee quickly.

I ran over, waving my arms, and screamed, "I'll take her from here! I'll take her!" I knelt down to Lily's level, let her smell me through all of her panting, and gently lifted her. Her breasts were engorged with milk as if she hadn't fed her puppies in a while, and she was shaking. Shaken myself, I was able to successfully transfer her into a crate in my car as we waited for her puppies to come out.

After a whole hour of being there, a little boy came out, carrying five itty-bitty puppies in a towel. I had been texted a picture of Lily and *seven* puppies nursing earlier.

"Where are the other two puppies?" I asked, pointing to the photo on my phone.

"We gave them away," the boy replied. So as not to startle the little boy, who could not have been older than seven, I asked him to get his mother.

"Where are the other two puppies?" I asked her once she arrived. "Your son just told me you gave them away. They'll die without their mother (or relevant proper care) at such a young age." Her face remained blank, so I started begging. "You need to get them back for me. Please." All I cared about was getting this little canine family out of there safely. After listening to me plead, the mom nodded, took out her phone, and made a call. She spoke quietly and in a different language, blocking her mouth with her hand. Something wasn't right.

Eventually, two teen boys came from across the street holding a towel. They walked over and unwrapped the towel to reveal one tiny puppy. I quickly reunited him with his mama, not knowing how long it had been since this puppy had eaten. The puppy latched on immediately, gulping down milk like his life depended on it, because it did.

"How long until the seventh puppy gets here?" I asked, trying to keep my cool.

"Oh," she said. "He died."

"*What?* What do you mean? Your son just told me you gave him away."

The woman standing in front of me was far too calm for the situation. She was unsympathetic and nonchalant, like the life of an innocent puppy meant nothing to her. It took everything in me to keep from snapping.

"We lied to him," she said. "That was his favorite puppy, and we didn't want to upset him."

It was impossible to know for certain whether or not this woman was telling the truth after all that had happened. I excused myself and called Mutt Scouts to explain the situation. They were skeptical as well. Examining the photo we were sent of the litter, we noticed that the puppy they claimed had passed was the only spotted one. It seemed all too suspicious—perhaps the spotted one being his favorite puppy was true and they were trying to keep it? Regardless, Mutt Scouts advised me to leave with Lily and the puppies I had before the family changed their mind.

For a week after, we called the family, their neighbors, and anyone else we could think of, trying to figure out if the puppy had actually passed or if they were just hiding it from us. We were confident that if this puppy hadn't already passed away, it would soon if we couldn't reunite him with his mama.

Eventually, we found out that they were, in fact, telling the truth. The puppy had died, probably from neglect, which is what happens when you're uneducated about how to care for such young puppies. I felt horrible. Would it still be alive if I had just come sooner? Even with six puppies and their mom safe and sound, it was still so easy to focus on the negative. Lily had lost one of her precious puppies. I could relate to how Riley felt when one of Madonna's puppies was stillborn. In the days that were to follow, I had to constantly remind myself that six of the seven puppies plus Lily was considered a good turnout in rescue.

Within a few hours of having Lily home, it was obvious she had been someone's pet: her coat was soft, her teeth pearly white, and she was the happiest, friendliest dog. She knew the name Lily, given to her by the family who found her, which inspired me to name her puppies after trees and flowers. Oak, Petunia, Marigold, Dahlia, Primrose, and Magnolia became the "Flower Children."

The first day with a new litter of puppies always makes me giddy. I start by weighing each puppy (which I'm sure you know by now is one of my favorite things to do), assigning them a colored collar, naming them, and photographing them to introduce them on social media. I typically decide on the litter theme ahead of time and brainstorm a scrolling list of names in the notes section of my phone. Then I run those names by the Mutt Scouts team to eliminate names that have already been used. This usually cuts my list in half. I'm always so indecisive on which puppy should have which name and color. What color looks best on them? Which name suits them best? Is there

any way I can make it easier for people to remember who is who? It's a whole process—but these are the questions I ask myself, which makes me love the process even more.

For the month and a half that Lily and the Flower Children lived with me, she followed me around wherever I went, even if she was in the middle of nursing. Lily loved plush toys and hoarded them in her bed or by her side on the couch. It was the cutest thing, but it also pointed to the fact that most likely she never had belongings like toys or cozy blankets. Lily and I worked together to improve her maternal skills. Lily was straight out of a chaotic episode of *Teen Mom*. She was very young, and for her, caring for her puppies was not her priority. As with all my mama dogs, we were a team and our job was to raise healthy puppies. That meant monitoring feedings closely, even if I had to sit by her side late into the night to keep her still in order to nurse her puppies.

Lily—now renamed Truffle—and the Flower Children were all adopted. We found seven loving homes for them, many of which were with owners who had never had a dog in their adult life. A few of the littermates recently had a reunion, and they recognized

each other immediately, playing for over an hour. It's always so fun attending litter reunions because I get to see how these puppies have transformed their adopters' lives. They're usually tired from raising puppies, but they're happy, and their hearts are full. The adopters always compare notes, telling stories about their puppies' little milestones, the funny thing they did the other night, and comparing then and now photos. Here's one I took from the reunion— their heads were bigger than their bodies were when I first rescued them.

WARNING: Do not raise newborn puppies at home without proper research, resources, and ample time to commit. Raising young puppies is a big-time commitment and an even bigger responsibility. If you find a litter of puppies, contact a local rescue for help. Even if you want to raise them, you can foster them with the support of the right rescue. Pet stores don't always carry all the supplies you need, like formula, syringes, and newborn puppy bottles, so hopefully a rescue can help you obtain them. With experience comes resources, so be open to help from those who've done it before.

WILLA AND VANESSA WILLIAMS

My dog rescue story involves a real-life superhero! We are talking Batman's partner in fighting crime . . . Robin. Yes, Burt Ward, who starred in the colorful 1960s *Batman* TV series that I grew up on, is the wonderfully dedicated owner of Gentle Giants, a big-dog rescue in Norco, California. And that's where we, as a family, fell in love with Dee Dee, a fawn-colored female Great Dane, roughly one and a half years old. Dee Dee was the first Dane they paraded out to us for review while we sat on a cold plastic bench with bated breath. Tracy Ward, Burt's wife, warmly greeted us after we passed a rigorous vetting system before we even showed up in person. She told us that a special girl, Dee Dee, was standing by the door, eagerly waiting to meet us. Then she brought her out. What a beauty! There were at least twelve more dogs who followed, getting bigger, goofier, and drippier with slobber, including an adorable brindle mastiff puppy. But we couldn't stop thinking about that graceful girl who came out first.

Now, how did we make the leap from our family's little five-pound Yorkie, Enzo, to a Great Dane? While I was shooting the TV series *Ugly Betty* in Hollywood, my costar America Ferrera showed up at our Raleigh Studios set with a Dane called Lucy. Lucy was a mantle Great Dane without a definite age, but she was big and sweet. America told me about Gentle Giants and how easy it was owning a Dane. I had always loved the idea of having a Great Dane but assumed they would immediately wreck my house and need endless exercise. But our Willa taught us otherwise. My daughter Melanie chose the name Willa for Dee Dee because it sounded more regal, and the character I played on the *Ugly Betty* series was named Wilhelmina. Willa soon became a regular in my trailer at Raleigh.

That's not the only set on which Willa starred. I brought her while I shot *Desperate Housewives* on Wisteria Lane, backstage at the Stephen Sondheim Theatre while I acted in *The Trip to Boun-*

tiful, and she stunningly posed in an *InStyle* shoot. She did have a crooked ear and would shiver and shake in fear when men were around, but eventually she learned to trust, relax, and give great hugs and kisses on her hind legs.

They say Great Danes have a short life span, but our Willa lived almost twelve years. Rescue dogs can send gratitude straight to your heart through their thankful eyes.

FACT

Contrary to popular belief, many large dog breeds are better suited to apartment living than smaller dog breeds. Great Danes and Bernese mountain dogs, for example, are known as gentle and easygoing breeds. Give them an hour of exercise, and they'll love to be curled up on the couch next to you the rest of the day.

It's a love that is so deep and satisfying. And since Willa, I have been a mom to four more Great Danes. I'm hooked. Long live dogs.

— Vanessa Williams

Nine

FAIRY TAILS DO COME TRUE

THERE'S A HOME
FOR EVERYONE

Fostering doesn't always equal cute puppies.

In fact, my most memorable foster experience thus far was a shy five-year-old dachshund mix named Cosmic who came from a severe hoarding case. She had come to me after struggling to open up at a previous foster's home. When she arrived, she had just thrown up all over herself in the car and smelled like sour milk. You could tell how shy and innocent she was right away. I was determined to make her come around. Once I set her down in the dog run on the side of my house, she immediately started sniffing and found a good spot to pee. I excitedly texted Amelie the good news: She peed! Never in a million years did I think I would be so enthusiastic about dog pee and poop, but for a dog with trauma, it indicates that they're getting comfortable—a great start to becoming a "normal" dog.

After giving Cosmic a few days to settle in, I decided to tackle her biggest fear: leash walking. She wasn't afraid of the sounds on the street and had no signs of leash aggression (friendly dogs can become triggered by being on a leash, causing them to lunge at other dogs and behave unpredictably). Instead, she was strangely scared of the leash itself. After fifteen minutes of playing hide-and-seek around the kitchen island each day, Cosmic would give in, cowering as I clipped the leash on her. I would carry her out onto my quiet dead-end street with a bag of Trader Joe's grated sharp cheddar cheese, which

I labeled "Cosmic's Cheese." For ten minutes, three times a day, I threw one shred of cheese at a time ahead of Cosmic and let her tiptoe toward it. On super-sunny days, the pieces of cheese that Cosmic left behind would melt on the asphalt, and neighborhood dogs would come lick it off. After a few days, my neighbor across the street started to come out just to see Cosmic's progress and cheer her on.

The progress was very, very slow, just like Cosmic's walking while on leash. Amelie and I were about ready to limit her to adopters with yards until I got a message from a woman named Ali on Instagram asking if Cosmic was still available. Within minutes of telling her yes, Ali had submitted an application. I poked around her Instagram, admiring pictures of her current dog, Sunny. Sunny and Cosmic had the exact same silhouette, but Sunny was tan and Cosmic was black and tan. They made for a picture-perfect match. Something was telling me that this was Cosmic's family.

When the day came around for Cosmic to meet Ali, her husband, and Sunny, I was so nervous. Another potential adopter, a kind schoolteacher, had visited Cosmic the day prior and Cosmic had shown no interest in her. However, when Ali and her husband arrived and sat down next to Cosmic, it was like she was a different dog. She approached Ali on her own and even let her scratch her belly, something she hadn't even let me do after living with me for two weeks! Pretty quickly Cosmic and Sunny were running around like they'd been sisters their whole lives. Within just fifteen minutes, it was clear that Cosmic was meant to join this family. Ali picked Cosmic up, replaced her Mutt Scouts collar with a new collar, and put a leash on her like it was nothing. I was stunned. Contrary to popular belief when it comes to fostering, I wasn't sad at all to see Cosmic go. I was incredibly moved by the whole experience and excited for her to start this new chapter in her life where she wouldn't be afraid anymore. I knew Ali and her husband could help her grow in a way that I wasn't able to. Within hours of sending Cosmic to her new home, I received pictures of Cosmic—now renamed Maya—cuddling with her sister, Sunny, grinning from ear to ear, and—get this—walking on a leash. I love when adopters send photo updates. It makes all the hard work completely worth it.

MAYA AND ALI LUNDBERG

We had the opportunity to meet Maya (at the time, Cosmic) through an incredible organization, Mutt Scouts, that does tremendous cross-border work rescuing dogs in need of a second chance. We met her at Victoria's home, and it was truly one of those love-at-first-sight moments. She has brought the greatest joy to our family and was by far the brightest spot of the pandemic. She quickly found her stride along her new pup sister, Sunny, and the two are the cutest kindred spirits. Quite often during the first few weeks after bringing Maya home, my husband and I would look at each other with the biggest smiles on our faces and say it feels like she was destined to be with us. The way she seamlessly adapted and then quickly began thriving in our home made it seem like she had been our pup forever. And forever is how long we will take the best care of her. Maya's adorable ways and infectious energy are a blessing, and we are so grateful that we have the opportunity to be her parents.

— *Ali Lundberg*

RECIPE
Celebrate Your Dog! Cake

Adopting a dog is something to celebrate! You're welcoming a new member into the family. Have a welcome-home party! Introduce your new dog to the neighbors and their dogs.

FOR THE CAKE

I large egg

2 tablespoons unsalted all-natural peanut butter (with no xylitol)

2 tablespoons melted coconut oil

¹/₄ cup apple sauce

¹/₂ can organic unsweetened pumpkin puree

2 tablespoons honey

I cup all-purpose flour

¹/₂ teaspoon baking soda

¹/₂ teaspoon baking powder

FOR THE FROSTING

I cup plain Greek yogurt

Drizzle of maple syrup

2 tablespoons unsalted all-natural peanut butter (with no xylitol)

Sprinkle of cinnamon

Organic food color of your choice

OPTIONAL DECORATIONS

Dog biscuits

Bacon

Blueberries (fresh or freeze-dried)

Kibble

Dog jerky sticks

1 Preheat your oven to 350 degrees Fahrenheit. Grease an 8 x 8–inch cake pan.

2 Whisk together the egg, peanut butter, coconut oil, apple sauce, pumpkin puree, and honey in a mixing bowl. Fold in the flour, baking soda, and baking powder with a rubber spatula—the batter will resemble a dough consistency rather than traditional cake batter.

3 Transfer cake batter to the prepared pan. Bake for 20 to 30 minutes. Let your cake cool while you make the frosting.

4 Combine all of the frosting ingredients in a mixing bowl. Frost the cooled cake and decorate as you wish!

Ten

LEAVING CAN BE RUFF

TRAVEL TIPS, TRICKS, AND ROAD TRIPS

Rue's small size was a key selling point in convincing my parents to cosign her adoption papers.

I assured them I'd take her wherever I went. I always bought all the carriers—the airline-approved bag, the sling you wear across your chest, and the breathable doggy backpack, too. After adopting Echo six months later (and being assured that he'd only be thirty pounds maximum), I figured the ease of traveling would remain. However, as I already mentioned, the rescue only predicted one-third of Echo's size; he ended up growing into a beautiful ninety-

pound dog that, at times, hikers have humorously mistaken for a wolf. By this time, it was too late to alter expectations of traveling with my dogs, so I was committed to making it work. I asked for a dog trailer that attached to my bicycle for my birthday, but after a sweaty ride from my apartment in Chelsea on Twentieth Street up to Central Park (about forty blocks) with Echo and Rue in tow, that thing never left my storage unit again. Eventually it was given to Maysie's mom Anne who used it as a big stroller when their black lab, Hope, could no longer walk due to old age.

I became a big fan of the Instagram account @bagdogs and would attempt silly things I'd seen, like cutting four leg holes in an IKEA shopping bag so I could take Echo on the subway.

"The MTA website only says your dog needs to be in a bag. It doesn't say you have to be *carrying* the bag," I would say to the subway attendant looking down at Echo wrapped in IKEA blue.

Unlike the MTA, Metro-North was more dog friendly. I rode it with Echo and Rue to my parents' house upstate monthly so they could have open space to run around. By the time they were two years old, Echo and Rue had been in cars, subways, trains, and even on a ferry.

After graduating from college, I moved from Manhattan to Los Angeles for the summer with my best friend, Gabby, so I could work at *Jimmy Kimmel Live!* There was no way I could leave Echo and Rue for an entire summer, and I hadn't yet figured out the ins and outs of traveling with dogs outside the state of New York, so we decided to drive across the country. Over the next ten days, Gabby, Rue, Echo, and I had a blast. We stopped in Nashville where Rue swam for the very first time, went all through Texas where we paddle boarded, and visited the first-ever membership bar and dog park in Texas, ate the spiciest burrito ever in New Mexico, and conquered the Grand Canyon with Echo by my side and Rue on my back on one of the hottest days of our lives. (Echo used the water fill-up stations as a sprinkler to cool off more than once.) Having the dogs with us for this epic road trip made it all the more adventurous. We drove every other day and found breathtaking hikes to tire out the dogs on our off days.

Dog Travel Checklist

- ◯ The food your dog eats

- ◯ Food and water bowls, plus a filled water bottle just for your dog. Your dog needs to stay hydrated, too!

- ◯ Leash, harness, and collar with all appropriate tags (e.g., ID, license, and rabies tags)

- ◯ Lots of poop bags! Respect the places you're traveling to.

- ◯ Treats to use as positive reinforcement for new situations

- ◯ Your dog's favorite toys and bones

- ◯ A dog bed or crate to ensure your dog will be comfortable

○ Pee pads. Even if your dog doesn't use these, it's always good to have them on hand in case an outdoor space isn't available. These pads have a subtle, artificial grass or urine scent to encourage dogs to go. I've brought Echo and Rue to the airplane bathroom and put a pee pad down for them to relieve themselves during long flights.

○ Towels. You never know what kind of mess you'll need to clean up.

○ Medication. Whether holistic or prescribed by your vet, it's always good to have something for nausea and anxiety on hand for your dog when traveling.

○ Any paperwork required by the airline. I always have my dogs' rabies certificates on hand, whether printed or on my phone.

Oftentimes, these hikes would end with Echo in need of a bath. In Santa Fe, New Mexico, a local told Gabby and me to hike at a ski basin that was closed for the summer. We followed our navigation, which led us farther and farther up the mountain, until we eventually lost service. Luckily, there was a fireman parked by the side of the road who, we discovered after pulling up behind him, had stopped to take a whiz. (Whoops!) After zipping his fly, he told us to just keep driving up and we would hit the basin. At a nauseat-

ingly high altitude, we parked in an empty lot and hit the slopes by foot. During the entire hike, we only briefly saw one woman, whom we will forever refer to as the "ghost of Santa Fe." Unsurprisingly, Echo found the smelliest pile of cow manure and rolled in it until his coat had turned from white to black. The manure was undeniably potent and caked into his long fur.

After completing the hike, we had no choice but to put Echo back in the car for the ride down. Even with all the windows open, our eyes teared from the smell. We pulled up to our La Quinta hotel (the best hotel chain in all the land—the comfiest beds, free coffee and waffles, and no dog fee; I always stay in a La Quinta on a road trip. Casey—a college friend who'll appear in chapter 13—wasn't lying) and took Echo straight to the bathtub. All we had was a tiny bar of hotel soap with minimal suds. Gabby and I took turns scrubbing Echo until our fingernails were filled with manure. The entire room reeked of Echo's mistake, and his thick fur clogged the bathtub drain. We left a generous tip for the cleaning staff, grabbed our things, and packed up the car. La Quinta: Gabby, Echo, and I sincerely apologize for the mess you had to deal with that day.

If it weren't for Echo and Rue, this road trip would've been a completely different (certainly cleaner) experience. Their influence has forever changed the way I travel, the parks and beaches I scope out, and how I admire nature and appreciate everything. Whenever a trip is presented to me, I ask myself, *How can I bring the dogs?* and go from there, because let's face it—they're coming. During the eight years of Rue's and Echo's lives, they've traveled every which way. They've jet-setted across the country over a dozen times now and have visited more states in America than your average human citizen! I can't wait to see the world through Alfie's eyes next.

Tips and Tricks for Traveling with Your Dog

Here are my tips and tricks for traveling successfully with your dog:

STAY CALM. This is perhaps the most important tip of all. Your dog can sense your energy. For example, If you're taking your dog on the plane with you (I do not recommend storing them underneath the plane with the luggage, as there's no guarantee it's temperature controlled) and you're nervous about how the cabin pressure will affect them on their first plane ride, they will be, too.

FAMILIARITY. Pack what they're used to. Traveling can be a stressful experience for newbie dogs, so you want to ease their stress by bringing along some familiar things. If they're used to sleeping in a crate, bring their crate no matter how heavy it is. Always pack more than enough dog food so you don't run out of their usual brand. Bring their favorite toy and maybe even their dog bed to set by your bedside.

MAKE IT EXCITING. This might sound contradictory to the previous tip, but if the travel duration is long and you're worried your dog will get impatient, buy them some new toys and a fresh bone. (I say fresh and not new because you don't want to try any new flavors in case they upset their stomach. A queasy dog is the last thing you need while traveling.)

TALK TO YOUR VET. Consider speaking with your vet about prescribing anxiety, sleeping, and/or nausea medication to have as backup. It's always best to be prepared!

EXPLORE ALTERNATIVE MEDICINE. If you'd rather go an au naturel route, visit the holistic section of your pet supply store and explore lavender dog treats, thunder vests, and other alternatives. A thunder vest got Rue through many crowded places. And a scoop of sugar-free canned pumpkin from the grocery store on top of their food will settle an upset stomach.

HAVE NO EXPECTATIONS. Like in life, we often have expectations that lead to disappointment. Just like kids, dogs can be unpredictable in unknown surroundings. Go with the flow.

DON'T FEEL GUILTY. When I first traveled with my dogs, I experienced a lot of guilt about inconveniencing other people. No matter how well-behaved your dogs are, there will always be people giving you looks as if what you're doing is wrong. Traveling with your dog is your right, and there are people who'll show you support and offer their help.

BE POLITE. While you may love dogs, another person may not. Always be considerate of other people's spaces and preferences. Sometimes when I fly, I'm seated next to someone who doesn't like dogs. Instead of being offended, I ask the flight attendant if one of us can switch, and I usually end up sitting next to a very nice dog lover who pets Echo the entire time and thanks me for helping pass the time.

SCOPE OUT HIKING SPOTS AND DOG PARKS AHEAD OF TIME. Anywhere I go with my dogs, I always research the best hikes, dog parks, and sometimes even beaches or lakes to take them to. It's a great opportunity to tire your dog out and meet the locals. I always leave the dog park with at least one amazing restaurant recommendation.

BE CREATIVE. Forgot a water bowl? Use a plastic takeout container. Need more toys? Consider cutting a tennis ball slightly along the seam to create a flap and stuff it with peanut butter or kibble (see page 115). Raining? Take your dog for a car ride—half of the excitement for Echo, Rue, and Alfie when traveling is the drive there. There will always be things you forget or bumps in the road, but enjoy the ride!

Then there are the times you can't take your dogs with you. I once nannied for a family who had interviewed sixty-eight people before hiring me. At the time, I thought that was beyond overkill. But recently, when I had to travel for work and couldn't bring my dogs with me, I started asking my mother to fly across the country to watch them. Without my mom's help, I'm actually not sure interviewing even sixty-eight dog sitters would have sufficed.

Since adopting Rue and Echo, a strong mutual attachment has developed. As I write this, we're all quite literally attached—Echo's head is on my foot (but if I dare move it, he'll burst up in fear because he's always been afraid of feet), and Rue's little sleeping body is perfectly following the curvature of my side. These dogs have been with me through college graduation, heartbreaks, and countless firsts. They moved to a house with me five times, back and forth between coasts when I couldn't make up my mind. They've been on their best behavior during first-date introductions, and they continue to be the shoulders I cry on at night and the belly laughs I need to set my day in motion each morning. Little Alfie now joins Rue and Echo. On a recent drive to San Diego, he insisted on balancing on the middle console (I know, not the safest, but oh so cute) so he could rest his head on my shoulder as he dozed off. For these reasons and more, I bring my dogs wherever I can, but sometimes, when they just aren't allowed, it's "Grandma" to the rescue.

As you may remember, my mom wasn't a dog lover until I converted her. Now she ships us all the latest doggy gadgets (Echo is still trying to figure out the automatic fetch machine she got him for Christmas) and hops on the plane whenever I need her to take care of my beloved pups and put my mind at ease. I don't know who has more separation anxiety—me or the dogs. They're certainly not watching me regularly on a camera that connects to their phone from anywhere in the world! And I know I'm not alone. Some pet owners are now spending a whopping $250 on a device that notifies them if their pet even glances at the camera and enables you to dispense a treat at the push of a button. If Echo and Alfie knew they could get treats just by looking at the camera, they would take doggy selfies all day.

Rue could not be more different. While I'm away, she pees on the edge of the carpet, takes all day to eat, and refuses to get out of my bed. She's the smallest biggest bed hog and is just as difficult to get out of bed as a pubescent teenager, but I wouldn't have it any other way. Eight years sleeping beside Rue and we've begun to mirror each other—lying on our side with our heads on the pillow, sheets tucked under our arms. It's difficult to sleep without her, and I'm so glad when Alfie joins us most nights as well. (But if my parents are in town, he always wants to sleep with them, and they love/hate it.) I once dated a guy who hated dogs in the bed (please tell me you don't agree), and I should've taken that as a red flag because he ended up being the sort of guy who breaks up with you over text. A dog would never do that. I'd choose Rue, Echo, and Alfie over a guy any day (except maybe Charlie Puth, my celebrity crush that no one gets. He has a rescue dog, too).

I love to travel, but I can't wait to come home when I'm away from the dogs for even a few days. To save time, I rarely check a bag, I order an Uber as soon as I get off the plane, and I rush out to meet my driver. The ride from the airport feels like forever; in those moments, the Los Angeles traffic irritates me more than usual. When I finally arrive, busting open the door like a scene from an action film, Rue, Echo, and Alfie emerge from my bedroom upstairs. I can see their heads peeking through the railing and the look in their eyes when they realize it's me. The cutest trio comes running down the stairs, Echo tripping over himself at least once, jumping for joy. I've been through it all to clear my acne-ridden skin, but I miss them so much that I end up letting them lick my face all over anyway.

FACT

Ever wonder if your dog actually knows how long you've been gone? Dogs tell time through their sense of smell. They're able to smell the time of day by how the environment changes as the sun shifts. As your scent gets weaker, they're able to get a sense for how long you've been away.[6]

When I get home from trips, I can't wait to spoon with Rue at night, and wake up in the morning to watch Echo swim for his ball in the pool, and chuckle at Alfie's unpredictable ears. Will they be up or down? Every morning they're different.

"Hey! Didn't you miss me?!" my mom will ask. Never in a million years would elementary-school me, sprinting from the school bus into my mom's arms, think I could ever be more excited to see anyone else. From greeting me with open arms at the edge of the driveway after school so I wouldn't have to carry my scoliosis-inducing, textbook-filled backpack an extra second to flying from New York to Los Angeles

---

6   Mary Jo DiLonardo, "Can Dogs Tell Time?" Treehugger, October 26, 2018, https://www.treehugger.com/can-dogs-tell-time-4862285.

to spoil Rue, Echo, and now Alfie with broiled salmon and long hikes every day while I'm away, my mom has always gone the extra mile for me. I definitely get my worrying tendencies from her, so I'm so glad I don't have to interview sixty-eight dog sitters. I can travel knowing Mom is taking care of everyone and everything as usual, waiting for me to come home.

DIY
Turn a Tennis Ball into a Food Puzzle

Keeping my dogs occupied while I'm gone, or even when they are traveling on long road trips or flights with me, can be tricky. Toys that involve food always keep my dogs occupied for much longer. The food keeps my dogs engaged while the "puzzle" is mentally stimulating and can minimize bad behavior due to boredom. Toss these tennis balls to your dogs on your way out the door, pack them, or make one on the go!

THE U-SHAPED TENNIS BALL: Using a knife, cut along the seam of an old tennis ball to make a U shape. (Be extremely careful since you're inserting the blade into the ball toward the hand holding it. Too many people visit emergency rooms in the US for cutting their hand while de-pitting an avocado or slicing a bagel.[7] We do *not* need the next reason to be because you were reading *Pup Culture* and Victoria told you to dig a knife into a tennis ball.) When you squeeze the cut tennis ball, the U should pop up. Fill the inside of the tennis ball with your dog's favorite kibble mixed with peanut butter, and freeze it.

THE X-SHAPED TENNIS BALL: If you're in a pinch and don't have time to wait for peanut butter to freeze, cut a small X in the tennis ball. When you squeeze the tennis ball, the X should pop open with a big enough hole to slip treats or kibble inside. Fill the tennis ball and let your dog have a ball!

7   Karen Miner, "The Surprising Reason These Foods Send People to the Emergency Room," Mashed, October 19, 2018, https://www.mashed.com/135913/the-surprising-reason-these-foods-send-people-to-the-emergency-room/.

Eleven

I'VE GOT A BONE TO PICK

--- 🐾 ---

SPAY AND NEUTER YOUR DOGS

Rescue is the only business that would be thrilled to be put *out* of business.

In an ideal world, everyone would spay and neuter their dogs, the millions of dogs in shelters would be adopted, and breeders could exist uncontroversially. Unfortunately, the world is not ideal in this respect.

My foster Cindy, a terrier mix with huge bunny-like ears, was rescued from the streets of Mexico. At the time, she was with her litter of grown puppies who had intense skin infections and were feral. This litter was under a year old, and she was already pregnant with another litter—four girls and six boys. I named them the Charcuterie litter— Salami (now Alfie Salami Shaffer; we're getting to his story), Apricot, Honeycomb, Chutney, Apple, Colby, Walnut, Fig, Almond, and Brie—since charcuterie boards were so trendy during COVID quarantine. I even sub-

mitted their picture to Chrissy Teigen's charcuterie board contest on Instagram. (We didn't win . . . but we should have!)

I didn't do live puppy weigh-ins with this litter, because I was concerned a few might not make it, though thankfully they all did. Many of the Charcuterie puppies were weak, and Salami, now Alfie, was an even more precarious case: he was born with a cleft paw and one leg shorter than the

Baby Alfie

other three. Their sweet, affectionate mom, Cindy, was also in bad shape. She was thin with a long, skinny neck like a giraffe's, and her skin sagged nearly to the ground with bald spots all over.

One evening I came home with my friend Courtney to find Cindy not acting like her usual friendly self. She didn't get out of bed to greet us, and after we finally persuaded her to get up and walk, her head drooped lower and lower with each step. Courtney and I both could tell that something was off. Her puppies came running up to nurse, but she did everything she could to get away from them. I would've accepted this behavior from my earlier foster teen dog mama, Lily, but never from Cindy.

Suddenly, I saw Cindy's eyes roll into the back of her head as she began to tremble. I thought she was having a seizure. Thanks to a FaceTime call, our vet was instantly able to diagnose Cindy with mastitis, an extremely painful bacterial infection of the breasts where the milk ducts can get clogged. One of Cindy's teats was as hard as a rock, and she would flinch in terrible pain every time a puppy would crawl over her or try to latch. We started Cindy on antibiotics and anti-inflammatory medication right away to ease her pain, but unfortunately, the antibiotics meant she could no longer nurse her puppies.

I rallied some friends and neighbors to come help bottle-feed her ten very hungry puppies that same evening. Try as we might, nobody could get a puppy to latch onto a bottle. We tried to feed the puppies using a plastic syringe, but they still refused—the gruel just dripped down their faces and all over our clothing. It was like the puppies were on a hunger strike, knowing that their mama was just in the other room and we wouldn't let them nurse. Cindy and her puppies whined and cried through the walls like call-and-response. It was excruciating to hear, but we knew it was for their own good.

The puppies' attitudes and appetites did not improve the next morning. They still refused to eat, and I was running out of options fast. There was no way Cindy was going to be able to feed her puppies. Mastitis typically takes two to three weeks to clear up, and the puppies were going to be old enough to eat on their own and get adopted before Cindy could fully recover. The only option was a heartbreaking one: we had to completely separate Cindy from her puppies by sending her to another foster home.

That evening, Courtney and I drove Cindy to another trusted Mutt Scouts foster willing to take her immediately. Cindy knew it was much too early to be leaving her puppies; she did everything she could to try to stay with them. She ran around the house, crying and panicking, making it very difficult to catch her. I felt like the worst person in the world, but the only way her puppies would eat is if they couldn't hear or smell Cindy nearby. Eventually, I was able to lift her and put her in the car. She yelped and cried, clawing at the door and trying to escape throughout the entire thirty-minute trip to her new foster home. It was brutal. When we brought her up to the door, she was obviously distressed and confused. My heart shattered into a million pieces. Her new foster family was very welcoming. They took her leash from me and I forced myself to drive off, casting one final glance at Cindy's little black nose, big ears, and scruffy face pressed between the rails of the porch banister.

When we returned without Cindy and brought a tray of gruel to the puppies, they ate on their own immediately. I was so relieved after nearly two days of the puppies eating little to nothing. I let them play outside extra long that evening in the hope they'd tire out and forget their mother was no longer there to cuddle them at night. The puppies slept through the entire night, thanks to their finally full bellies, but Cindy did not. Her new foster struggled to calm her down. She paced around the house all night, looking for her puppies and crying. In the morning, Cindy was found tracking blood all over, probably from stress and from birthing too many litters, and she was in obvious pain without her puppies able to drain her milk supply.

While I felt for Cindy and her puppies, there was no time to harp on it. I had a huge responsibility now—to raise ten puppies on my own. I geared up—human baby bottles, teensy newborn puppy bottles, plastic syringes, formula, canned food, soaked kibble, blender. These were my tools to get these puppies to eat every two to three hours, and I would do anything to ensure they did. I was committed to raising healthy and happy puppies, even without their mother.

For three weeks, I barely left the house. I spent all my time with the puppies. I wrote some of this book on the floor in the puppy pen with ten puppies scattered around me. Many of my meals were eaten standing up, and my Zoom calls always involved at least one puppy being soothed. Thankfully, Cindy recovered from her mastitis and got adopted into a loving home where she and her record-breaking ears became the center of their world.

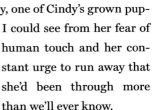

When the Charcuterie puppies were all adopted (except Alfie Salami . . . We're getting to his story—I promise), I ended up fostering Valley, one of Cindy's grown puppies we were struggling to find an adopter for. I could see from her fear of human touch and her constant urge to run away that she'd been through more than we'll ever know.

While Cindy, the Charcuterie litter, and eventually Valley got happy endings, I want to point out three alternative endings that could've very well happened if it weren't for rescue efforts.

Cindy (center left) and Valley (center) when they were first rescued

1. Without Mutt Scouts rescuing Cindy off the streets, the Charcuterie litter would have killed Cindy, because many of her puppies got stuck during birth.

2. If I hadn't been able to care for the Charcuterie litter when Cindy could no longer do so, these tiny puppies would have had a long and painful death from starvation if they hadn't already caught a virus (parvo, distemper, etc.) on the streets.

3. And lastly, without treatment, Cindy's mastitis could have led to a serious infection, causing her intense pain, or even death.

I want to convey these harsh truths to illustrate the importance of spaying and neutering and the harm you can cause if you neglect to do so. According to the animal overpopulation statistics provided by SNAP (Spay-Neuter Assistance Program), up to 508 puppies can be born from just *one* unspayed female dog and her offspring in seven years![8] Those are a lot of pups to rescue. If you cannot afford to fix your dog, search for low-cost or even free spay-and-neuter clinics in your area. They exist and are just a Google search away, so there are no excuses (for example, there's the Bark Avenue Foundation, an organization that offers free spaying and neutering in inner-city areas like Compton and East LA). In case you're still questioning whether to spay or neuter your dog, here are some facts that might convince you to do so:

- A fixed dog is less prone to diseases such as breast cancer, uterine disease, testicular disease, and prostate disease.[9]

- Spaying or neutering your dog is much cheaper than caring for a litter of puppies.

- If more people fixed their dogs, there would be fewer unwanted and stray dogs, and therefore, millions of dollars would not need to be spent on animal control. [8]

- There are approximately 670,000 dogs euthanized each year. Every puppy your dog has is responsible for taking a home away from a shelter dog in need. [5]

8   "Spay-Neuter Facts Overpopulation Facts," SNAP. https://www.snapus.org/spay-neuter-facts-overpopulation-facts/.
9   "Spay and Neuter," PETA, https://www.peta.org/issues/animal-companion-issues/overpopulation/spay-neuter/.

Do your part to help solve the overpopulation and suffering of dogs, for which humans are responsible. We made the problem; we can fix it.

Ten Vet Questions Answered by Dr. Gary Weitzman

1. How often should I groom my dog? Specifically, bathing, brushing, and trimming its nails? When is it best to turn to a professional groomer?

Grooming goes beyond keeping your pet clean. It helps you stay aware of any health concerns, like lumps, bumps, cuts, or other problems, so you can seek veterinary care early. Frequent brushing and bathing can even cut down how much hair ends up all over your house.

Some grooming, like brushing and combing, can be done at home. You can bathe your pet at home, too, but if the task seems too daunting, a professional groomer can bathe and dry your pet for you. If you own a breed that requires regular haircuts, you'll most likely want to enlist the help of a professional groomer, although you can also learn to do this yourself.

Some dog breeds require routine clipping and trimming. Poodles, shih tzus, Yorkshire terriers, Maltese, Portuguese water dogs, as well as many labradoodles, goldendoodles, and similar breeds should be clipped every four to eight weeks. If you don't have this done, the hair will just keep growing and growing, eventually developing unsightly and painful mats throughout the coat. Neglect grooming appointments, and your groomer might have no choice but to shave your dog down to the skin. No one wants that.

If you choose to groom your own dog, investing in the right equipment for your breed (clippers, clipper blades, scissors, a grooming table, and a pet dryer), is key, but it can also be pricey. However, professional grooming is also expensive, so the investment can be worth it. If you got your dog through a breeder, they might be happy to teach you how to groom your pet. Just ask!

There are many great grooming books available, including some for specific breeds. You can also watch YouTube videos on pet grooming to learn about safety and correct technique. But a word of caution: Grooming scissors are extremely sharp. Be careful that you don't accidentally cut your dog's delicate skin, and use caution when working around the face.

How often your dog will need a bath depends on a number of factors, including how dirty your dog gets and what type of coat it has. Choose a gentle, moisturizing shampoo, preferably one made with natural ingredients. I love oatmeal-based shampoos. There's no need for flea shampoo, because your dog's monthly flea preventive will take care of those intruders for you.

It's important to trim your dog's nails regularly to prevent overlong nails that snag on something and tear. Nails can also grow all the way around and end up embedded, painfully, in your dog's paw pads. Get your pup used to your placing his paws in your hand as a first lesson in the fun of getting a pedicure. Do this by touching his paw and giving him a tasty treat as a reward. Trim your pup's nails about every other week to once a month to keep them short and comfortable. Styptic powder can be applied to the nail with pressure to stop bleeding if you accidentally nick the quick (the vein in the nail). If you're dealing with black nails you won't be able to see the quick, so be very conservative and take off only the tips of the nails or let your veterinary technician or groomer do the nail trim for you.

2. Let's talk poop! Are there certain types we should look out for that are concerning?

Just like us humans, all dogs are different. But it's important to understand what's normal for your dog. Poop can reveal a great deal about your dog's health. Healthy dog poop should be compact, moist, and hold its shape when picked up. If it's runny or watery, this could be a sign of intestinal upset—maybe your dog has eaten something he shouldn't. Similarly, if the poo feels too hard or dry, your dog may be suffering from dehydration or constipation. If you notice a change in your dog's poo consistency, make sure to discuss it with your vet. If you've recently changed your dog's food, it's normal to expect some stool variation in the first few days, so don't panic. If things haven't settled down after two weeks, I recommend you consult your veterinarian.

The color of your dog's poop can tell us a lot. Anything other than light or dark brown—ideally a milk chocolate color—may be cause for concern. Dog food may contain some food colorings, too, so check the ingredients, as this may affect the color of your pooch's poop.

GREEN: This could be a sign of a gallbladder issue, or that your pup has been overeating grass, which could indicate stress or intestine troubles.

ORANGE/YELLOW: This could be a sign of an issue with the liver or pancreas, both of which will require veterinary attention.

RED: Red streaks generally mean there is blood in your dog's poop, which could be due to a cut near your pup's anus, so it's worth having a quick look.

BLACK/TARRY: Could be a sign of internal bleeding in the stomach or small intestines, which requires urgent attention.

GRAY/GREASY: May mean a pancreas or biliary issue, so get your dog checked out by your vet.

WHITE SPOTS: White, rice-like grains in your pup's poop could be a sign of tapeworms, which will require treatment.

WHITE/CHALKY: This is usually due to an excess of calcium and other minerals and is typically observed in dogs with a raw diet.

3. Why do dogs eat grass? Does it affect digestion?

Honest answer? Beats me. I can only guess that the strong smell of chlorophyll piques their interest enough to chow down. The good news is it's a completely harmless activity. The old adage that dogs eat grass to make themselves throw up is all backward. Sure, the grass comes first and the vomit second, but that's completely unintentional on their part.

4. What is the best way to introduce a new dog into my home if I already have pets? Does the type of introduction depend on what kind of pets I have or my existing dog's current age?

Whether you're bringing home a new puppy or kitten, cat or dog, hamster or rabbit, you need to introduce the newcomer to your other animals carefully. If it's another dog, you may have already done this at the shelter (or, better yet, tried it at home). In truth, we're a little wary of doing introductions at the shelter because it's such an abnormal environment for both animals. A better way is to do a first meeting on neutral ground for both dogs somewhere other than your home or the shelter. Regardless, there are a few basics to keep in mind.

First, go slow. For a new puppy or dog, be sure to keep both animals safe. That means a leash for both dogs, or at least for your current dog if you bring home a puppy who doesn't know about leashes yet. Be cautious until the animals get a good look at each other; then allow a little more contact until they're both safely playing happily together.

The most important thing you can do for your new pet is to give him his own safe space. This can be a quiet room, a corner of the den for a dog bed or open-door crate, or a cat tree in the living room, preferably underneath a sunbeam. Remember that your pet is getting used to his new human family as much as you're getting used to your new pet. If all goes well, your pet will never want to be in that quiet space without you nearby.

5. How can I help my new dog transition and adjust to my home? How long will it take for my dog, fostered or adopted, to decompress and feel comfortable?

You can take some easy steps to help your new pet get acclimated. Consistency is the single most important thing you can provide your new animal. It's not only the easiest way for new pets to learn but it's also the easiest way for you to become comfortable with them. Come up with a schedule for feeding, walks, playtime, and training, and stick to it.

Get the essentials out of the way by having everything up and ready before you bring your new dog or cat into the home. Would you invite human guests to stay with you and not stock the fridge with their favorite food or make their bed with fresh linens? Set up a crate and bed for your dog in a quiet, safe space. Stock up on toys, training treats, food, and bowls. Be organized from day one, and life will be easier for everyone. Oh, and don't vary the routine. You'll thank me for that when you start house-training.

You need patience to start a new relationship. It might be challenging, or even at times upsetting, sleep depriving, and nerve-racking. But what relationship isn't worth a little work and patience? Your new relationship will take time to develop—not just with regard to how you react to your pet, but how it reacts to you. In fact, chances are that your pet's true personality and behavior won't be evident for weeks or even months. But once you go through that initial gauntlet, it will lead to a long-term, no-comparison, beautiful relationship you'll never have wanted to miss.

6. What are my options for affordable pet health care? Is pet insurance worth it?

There are a number of affordable pet health care options. For example, San Diego Humane Society offers low-cost vaccines, microchips, and spay/neuter appointments. There are animal welfare organizations and rescue groups that offer low-cost or free routine care as well.

I strongly recommend pet insurance. Premiums are usually reasonable for puppies, kittens, and younger healthy adults. Plans cover illnesses, injuries, and prescriptions, as well as routine and preventive care, depending on the plan. Read your premium information carefully and even call the insurer to make sure you understand what is covered and what isn't. Alternatively, you can set up a medical fund for your pets, putting aside money every month, but in reality, most people don't follow through with this. Pet insurance provides peace of mind. Someday, if you really need it, it might be the smartest thing you've ever done.

7. My dog's breath stinks! How should I care for my dog's oral hygiene? How often do I need to brush its teeth? Should I be worried?

Imagine how you'd feel if you didn't brush your teeth every day. What if you skipped brushing for a week or even a month? What about an entire lifetime? Not only would your mouth be disgusting, but you would probably not have very many teeth left in your old age.

This is the reality for many pets. Very few pet owners brush their dog's teeth every day, but we should! Daily brushing is the best thing you can do for your pet's teeth and gums, but good dental care goes much further than that.

Dental disease is caused when bacteria in the mouth form plaque on the teeth. Plaque then hardens into calculus (also called tartar) above the gum line, where you can see it, and below the gum line, where you can't see it. Plaque and tartar under the gum line wreak havoc on your dog's or cat's mouth, leading to gum inflammation, bleeding, and tooth loss. Studies have shown that dental disease can even contribute to heart disease, liver disease, and kidney disease. And let's not forget horrible pet breath! It's not normal for your pet's mouth to have a terrible stench; if that's the case, it's time for a dental exam by your vet.

Plaque can be brushed away, but tartar can only be removed by a professional cleaning, much like the biannual cleanings you get from your own dentist. Still, you can space these professional cleanings out by brushing your pet's teeth at home, which will make a huge difference in the health of his teeth and gums. Brush at least every other day, although daily is best. After brushing, plaque starts re-forming within twenty-four hours. If you don't brush away plaque, it then hardens into tartar within three to five days.

To get started, you'll need a toothbrush and some pet toothpaste. Pet toothbrushes come in a few styles. Finger brushes are plastic tubes that fit over your finger with soft bristles on the tip. You can also use a pet toothbrush that looks more like your own, although pet toothbrushes have very soft bristles. Pet toothpaste comes in many flavors designed to entice your pet, including malt, vanilla, mint, and the ever popular poultry flavor. Never use human toothpaste; it'll make your pet sick.

To warm up, just let your puppy or kitten lick a dab of toothpaste.

Next, put a small amount of toothpaste on your finger and gently rub a few teeth. Praise your pet for cooperating. Go slowly, brushing a few teeth at a time, pausing to praise until the entire mouth is brushed. Graduate to a soft brush from here and you're on your way to a new world of pet dental hygiene.

Brushing your pet's teeth at home is the best way to keep his mouth healthy, but most pets still benefit from professional cleanings at least once every other year. Your vet or a trained veterinary technician will use special equipment to clean above and below the gum line. Often this equipment is an ultrasonic cleaner exactly like the one your dentist or hygienist uses on your teeth. Although the procedure is similar to what we have done at the dentist, pets are put under general anesthesia for dental cleanings. This is because they won't sit there and hold their mouths open while someone scrapes and cleans their teeth for thirty minutes.

Veterinary anesthesia is very advanced now and is safe under the careful eye of your veterinarian, even for senior pets. With good preparation, by which I mean an exam and a preanesthetic blood test to screen for any problems, your pet should be fine having this procedure. Always insist on IV fluids, especially for senior pets. This will flush the kidneys and clear the pre-gas anesthetics more quickly (the lungs will take care of the gas anesthesia).

Only a full dental exam and cleaning under anesthesia will reveal fractured teeth, painful erosions, or loose incisors. Animals don't tell us they're in pain until things get really ugly. Just think about what it's like to have tooth pain yourself. Do yourself and your pet a favor and plan on having a full dental procedure done every other year once your pet turns seven. Some pets need dental cleanings more frequently. Yorkies, toy poodles, shih tzus, and other small breeds: they're adorable but cursed with very high-maintenance dental needs.

8. Are there diseases that my dog can give me, and vice versa? (Coronavirus?)

At this time, there is no evidence that animals play a significant role in spreading the virus that causes COVID-19. Based on the limited information available to date, the risk of animals spreading COVID-19 to people is considered to be low.

Some coronaviruses that infect animals can be spread to humans and then spread between people, but this is rare. This is what happened with the virus that caused the current outbreak of COVID-19, the virus is now spreading from person to person.

Germs from dogs can cause a variety of illnesses, from minor skin infections to serious illnesses. One of the best ways you can protect yourself from getting sick is to thoroughly wash your hands after handling, caring for, feeding, or cleaning up after dogs. By providing your dog with routine veterinary care, cleaning up after your dog, and preventing dog scratches and bites, you're less likely to get sick from touching or interacting with a dog.

9. Are there things I should be doing while my dog is still young to prevent common health problems, such as joint issues like arthritis, obesity, cataracts, ear infections, and cancers?

Ask yourself this question: What makes my pet happy? Running, swimming, perching, stalking, and sniffing are all normal behaviors for our animal companions. Ensure your furry friend gets to do these as often as possible, and he will live a healthier and happier life.

You can't have a healthy dog without enrichment, and there's no such thing as enrichment without exercise. Exercise is critical to physical and mental health, helping with mobility, weight maintenance, and overall fitness. According to the Association for Pet Obesity Prevention, nearly 60 percent of cats and 54 percent of dogs in the United States are overweight or even obese. They, like us, need to hit the "gym" to stay healthy and happy.

Dogs should be outside exercising every single day. The best exercise of all is off-leash playing and running in a safe environment, whether that's a dog park, a ball field, or your backyard. If you don't have an easily accessible place to let your dog safely off leash, there are many other great options for both you and your dog. I'm a fan of long walks with a dog or with a human. Just do it. Get your dog out as often as possible. A tired dog is a good, happy, and healthy dog. As a routine, plan on a "business" walk at least twice a day; longer walks and hikes are great, but most of us can't count on those until the weekend.

A healthy diet sets the stage for a healthy lifetime. I'd be a happy camper if I could subsist on chips and peanut butter for the rest of my life, but my life might be significantly abbreviated if I got my wish. The same goes for your pet. Animals have definite nutritional requirements, and sometimes these are unique to species. These are facts you shouldn't ignore when considering what to feed your pet. Remember the Five Freedoms, the most basic care all animals deserve. One of those is "freedom from hunger or thirst," and it goes beyond simply providing food and water—your pet deserves much more than just the basics to survive.

Your veterinarian is your partner in your pet's health care, even when your pet is not sick. Let me rephrase that: *especially* when your pet is not sick. Visiting your vet for preventive care is just as important as going when your pet is ill or injured. In fact, staying on top of your pet's health when he's well can help spot diseases early so they can be treated fast. "An ounce of prevention is worth a pound of cure" doesn't apply only to humans.

Examining a pet annually records a baseline on which future exams can be compared; you have to know what's normal before being able to recognize what's not. For instance, you might just think your dog is acting odd but not be able to say exactly why. It's better if your vet can identify a physical difference in your dog based on what was normal the previous year.

As far as how often you should visit your vet, if you consider that one year for you is roughly equivalent to six or seven of your pet's years, the value of the physical exam is even more compelling. So, please, schedule a physical exam once a year, even if vaccines are not due. It will be the most valuable ounce of prevention you'll ever spend on your pet.

Many veterinarians offer wellness plans. Modeled somewhat on the human health maintenance organization model, these plans cover routine checkups, vaccines, dewormers, and some tests on a set schedule. The beauty of these plans is twofold: costs are lower overall, and you get an easy-to-follow schedule for checkups. Puppy or kitten packages are the most common wellness plans, but your vet might also offer young adult and senior wellness plans.

Some pet insurance providers also offer wellness insurance, which works like medical insurance, but instead of covering illnesses and injuries, it covers only preventive services, like vaccines, well visits, spaying or neutering, and dental cleanings. Such plans may be purchased individually or as an add-on to your pet's medical insurance.

With ear and eye problems, your pet's hearing or vision could be at stake, so don't delay making a veterinary appointment when you suspect something might be wrong. Although it's often easy to see when something is amiss in the eyes (squinting, tearing, redness, or discharge), the ears can be trickier, especially if your pet has floppy ears. Make a habit of looking inside your pet's ears every week or so just to make sure everything looks okay. Normal, healthy ears should look clean and smell pleasant. If you notice any redness, heavy debris, or discharge in or around the ear canal, or if you detect a foul odor, a vet visit is in order.

Pets who get frequent ear infections or a lot of buildup in the ears will benefit from weekly or biweekly ear cleanings. Start out with a big cotton ball (cotton batting is even better). Wet the cotton with the ear cleaner and use it to swipe out the inside of the ear. A small amount of cleaner will naturally drip down into the ear canal. Gently massage the base of the ear with your fingers. Stand back and let your pet shake his head (drape a towel over his head to minimize the mess). Then use the cotton ball to softly wipe out the ear. Never stick a cotton swab into the ear canal; you can rupture your pet's eardrum.

Spaying and neutering your pet (sometimes called "altering" or "fixing") are means of permanent birth control, ensuring your pet will never accidentally contribute to the pet overpopulation problem. Spaying and neutering also have some health benefits (including a decrease in certain cancers) and behavioral benefits for pets who live in a human world.

Spaying will lower or even stop the production of the female hormones estrogen, progesterone, and oxytocin. Neutering significantly cuts down on the production of testosterone. The absence of these hormones stops the development of secondary reproductive effects, such as mammary gland development, and eliminates the heat cycle in females. In males, neutering significantly decreases the incidence of prostate disease and entirely eliminates the possibility of testicular cancer (for obvious reasons). Similarly, spayed females can never get ovarian cancer.

10. I'm asking this question for my dog Echo, who suffers from allergies and irritated skin: Is it true that white dogs have more allergies and sensitivities than black or brown dogs?

Variations in coat color result from the amount of pigment a dog produces, which is determined by genetics. Dark-colored dogs produce more pigment than lighter dogs; white coat color results from a complete lack of pigment production. Even dogs of the same breed can have wide variations in their coat colors depending on their genetic makeup. Chocolate, black, and yellow Labradors, for instance, are often all born in the same litter.

Your dog can be affected by a variety of skin diseases, such as infections, immune-mediated processes, and skin allergies. Although no evidence says dogs with lighter coat colors are more prone to any of these types of skin diseases when compared to dogs with darker coats, in one category color variation becomes important. A difference exists in the risk of developing skin cancer between light- and dark-coated dogs. Dogs with lighter coat colors experience more sun damage to their skin and therefore are at higher risk of developing skin cancers that relate to sun exposure. In an interesting twist, dogs with dark coats are more at risk of developing melanoma, which is a tumor that arises from the cells that produce pigmentation.

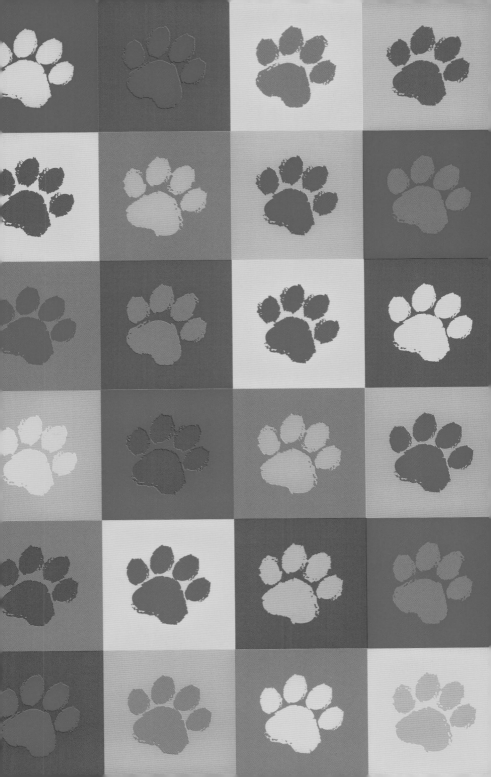

Twelve

PERFECTLY IMPERFECT

---- 🐾 ----

SPECIAL DOGS, SPECIAL NEEDS

Felix was my first special-needs foster and the first special-needs dog I've ever really gotten to know.

While Felix was with me, he made me feel like no problems were big problems and that every day should be appreciated. He has such a passion for life and stays positive despite his inability to run and keep up with other able-bodied dogs.

When I received a call asking if I would foster Felix, there was a "no pressure" precursor because Felix required around-the-clock care. He'd been hit by a car, injuring his spine and leaving him incontinent and paralyzed from the waist down. I thought, *If I can raise*

large litters of puppies, how hard could this be? I only realized after spending time with Felix that it was wrong to compare fostering him to raising puppies. Puppies gain strength and freedom, while Felix's were taken away.

When Felix arrived at my home, he was in much worse shape than I had envisioned. Seeing him drag his hind legs was obviously upsetting and difficult to get used to. The skin on the tops of his paws was peeling from the constant friction of being dragged, and the drastic curvature of his spine was like an S.

That first evening, I put a baby pool inside a playpen and filled it with cozy, fluffy blankets—a trick I learned from fostering puppies to protect my floors—and lifted him into it to sleep. I woke up in the middle of the night to a bunch of ruckus and ran downstairs. Turns out Felix didn't like sleeping in the baby pool and had managed to get his two front legs out enough to drag the pool, the playpen, and the other half of his fifty-pound body across the room. Half-asleep, I hoisted him out of the pool and brought him outside. He was soaked in his own urine and needed to be hosed off. It was cold and dark, but despite that, Felix seemed happy to be back in my presence. His green eyes beamed with joy as he dragged himself closer to me. I put a towel under his hips to help hold him up in a standing position so that I could hose him down. I reset his playpen, sans baby pool, and tucked him back in all clean and dry. He slept soundly the rest of the night.

The next morning I woke Felix up and put him in his wheelchair. I

was told he'd never had any desire to use it, but I was determined to give him some of his mobility back. Afraid that his little feet couldn't take any more dragging, I used all my strength to lift him into it and strap his limp legs in. As soon as I did, Felix took off running and jumping with the other dogs like it was no big deal. I was luckily able to capture his trotting and enthusiasm on camera and circulated it to the Mutt Scouts team. Everyone was crying happy tears. Rescue can be brutal. We see so many abused and ill dogs at the fault of humans, so when a breakthrough happens, no matter how small, we cherish it. It helps keep us going and reminds us why we do this day in and day out.

After seeing Felix's joyous will to live, it was decided he would go to a live-in rehab facility where he could get round-the-clock care and therapy to give him the best chance of walking again.

Leaving Felix at a live-in rehab was a big decision because it would cost Mutt Scouts so much to keep him there. Knowing, however, that it was the best option for him, I started a Facebook fundraiser for Felix, and I was able to raise enough money to cover the first week of his care. It's true—every penny truly helps. After just a week with Felix, I loved him so much. I really was rooting for his recovery. I believed and still believe that he'll regain continence and mobility because of his positive and persistent attitude. Felix may be special-needs, but he's also just plain special. He's still looking for an equally special owner who'll give him a happy life, and I'm confident that he'll find his patient, dedicated, and understanding forever home before too long. (Hopefully this book will touch sometime who will love and adopt him.)

Fostering Felix inspired me to work harder. Each morning I'd set up my phone to record me working with Felix to balance on all four legs. I'd study the video all day in hopes that the next day we could add a second or two to our time. I started fostering because I wanted to help dogs. Felix was the dog that made me feel most helpful, and I was addicted to that feeling. I knew I wanted to help another special-needs dog in the future, but I never expected that two months later, when Cindy and the Charcuterie litter came to my home, my forever special-needs boy would come so soon.

Nine of the ten Charcuterie puppies were adopted within two weeks, but nobody was interested in Salami, the puppy born with a

TIP

Many animal rehab facilities have a boarding option. Though difficult to part with your dog, having your dog live at the facility allows for intense rehabilitation (aqua therapy, acupuncture, etc.) that will hopefully give your dog faster results. Please note: boarding, whether rehab or training, can be extremely costly. Speak to your vet about options near you to decide if this course of action is the right one for you and your dog.

deformed left leg and paw. His unknown future was too risky for people. They would ask, "Is he going to need to have it amputated?" Nobody knew the answer. While living in Manhattan, I always thought two dogs were enough. Any more dogs would make tasks as common as walking down the crowded

sidewalk difficult. Once I moved to Los Angeles, where I was fortunate enough to have a backyard and a doggy door, I became open to the idea of adopting another dog. Each time I took in a new foster dog, I kept an open mind. Was this new foster going to be my third dog?

When the Charcuterie litter came to me, I didn't at all think my third dog was in that litter. But as time went on and their mom, Cindy, got sick, this litter grew to have a special place in my heart. I was responsible for feeding them, comforting them, and keeping them warm. I would rock two puppies to sleep at a time, one in each hand. I'd been Echo and Rue's mom for eight years, but now I was mom to ten more precious pups.

Salami was different. Not just because of his paw but also because he was unbelievably sweet and calm for a puppy. I never felt stressed in his presence. I pushed him on all my friends, hoping one of them would adopt him so he could still stay in my life. The truth is I didn't imagine my third dog would be a puppy, though I was convinced it would have special needs. A puppy seemed too adoptable to be my next dog. I had two beautiful, healthy, and well-behaved pets. I wanted my next dog to be a worthy challenge, in the sense that I wanted to truly feel like I made a difference in their life.

To my surprise, Salami was passed up again and again. His coat turned redder and redder as he got older, and he was the king of puppy-dog eyes. I was just smitten with that expressive little face and his goofy wobble. Salami had no idea he was born different. He was more confident, outgoing, and social than so many of the puppies I'd fostered. After seeing so many pass on Salami, I started to think maybe he was meant to be mine. It wasn't too long before I became the proud adopter of Salami, now Alfie Salami Shaffer, and love how unique his missing toes and short leg make him. I call him my cleft-paw cutie, and he's perfect in every way.

You'd think that a puppy as young and cute as Alfie would undoubtedly be adoptable, but it turned out that wasn't the case. His special need—if you can even classify his little leg and paw as a special need—deterred many adopters. He's cute to look at and play with, but the uncertainty in his future wasn't a risk people were willing to take. You see, by the time this book comes out, Alfie will have turned one. I have no idea what he'll look like or if he'll have four legs or three. What I am certain of, however, is my ability to help him lead a happy and full life no matter what the future holds.

Alfie roasts his first marshmallow

Just like special-needs dogs deserve loving homes yet often have difficulty finding them, senior dogs do, too. Sadly, most senior dogs once knew a home. Owner surrender is far too common, whether due to elderly owners' inability to care for their dogs anymore and having nobody to help, owners unable or unwilling to pay medical bills piling up, or worst of all, owners deciding they want to trade in their older dog for a puppy instead. Owning a dog means promising to take care of it for the entire duration of its life. Before you make this commitment, make a plan: Who'll take the dog if something were to happen to you? Everyone needs a backup plan. How will you pay if an emergency were to arise? Consider investing in health insurance for your dog early on or find low-cost clinics in your area.

Once a senior dog enters a shelter, it's often overlooked, even though it's the one most in need of getting out of there. A dog's likelihood of being adopted from a shelter drops sharply each year. A 2017 article from *The Dodo* says that seniors make up the bulk of the dogs put down at shelters every year in the US.

Imagine if your parents, home, and everything you knew were ripped from under you without warning and you were sent to a crowded, chaotic, unfamiliar place. The shelter can be extremely stressful and anxiety inducing for a senior dog who deserves to live out its days resting in a quiet and comfortable home. Giving a senior dog a new home means saving a life. It means endless cuddles and a constant companion by your side. By adopting a senior, you'll be adopting a dog who's grown into its personality, and you'll be more likely to get a sense of the dog's temperament, habits, and prior history.

If you have concerns regarding the medical costs of a senior dog, know that there are some nonprofit organizations and rescues that will help cover a senior dog's medical costs for the rest of its life if that dog finds a foster/

forever home. For example, The Grey Muzzle Organization provides funding and resources to animal shelters, rescue organizations, sanctuaries, and other nonprofit groups nationwide, and Frosted Faces is a nonprofit organization that rescues senior animals and rehomes them, as well as offers financial assistance to owners of senior pets. They also board senior dogs at an inexpensive rate while providing quality care.

Another thing to note is that many rescues have hospice programs for dogs with untreatable terminal illnesses (many of which are senior dogs). Hospice in this context means taking a dog into your home and giving it palliative care: love until it is its time to go.

If you can open your heart and home to foster or adopt a senior dog, I encourage you to scope out your local shelters, rescues, and other organizations to find the perfect, lovable senior dog for you.

Q&A with Dan Levy

VICTORIA SHAFFER: What inspired you to adopt a dog—specifically, an adult dog?

DAN LEVY: Well, I knew that I wanted to rescue a dog first and foremost, just because specifically in Los Angeles, there are so many dogs in need of homes. I also knew that I didn't want to jump into anything unless I had completely thought it through. So, I started to look on Petfinder at everything and anything—young dogs, old dogs—and I did it casually over about a year and a half. Then one day I discovered Redmond's little picture and scrolled through the photos and read the description.

They described him as, you know, very shy and quiet and low-key, which were all things that I was hoping for in a dog. So, I scheduled a visit to the foster home to look at him. The foster family sort of picked him up and, you know, I held up my hand and he put his head in it and completely fell asleep, and I knew from that moment on that he was going to be a part of the family.

So, yeah, it was a very gradual process, one that took a lot of time and care and thought.

V: His little head in your hand is the cutest image ever. After adopting an older dog, was there any special training or work you had to do to get him acclimated to your home and his new life?

D: When I first got Red, he spent the first twenty-four hours in my house behind a curtain and wouldn't come out. I didn't know what to do, because he would nip at me every time I tried to pet him. At first, I thought I had somehow adopted a very aggressive dog, or a dog that needed some kind of trauma training or deprogramming.

I went online and started to read about other people's experiences that were very similar to mine. The common solution was to outstretch your hand the minute they go to nip, tap them on the nose, and then immediately go in to pet their head.

And I tried it and it worked. From that point on, he was acclimatized. I mean, it took him a couple of days to get used to the space, but that trick really worked. I guess it was just, you know, asserting dominance, making him comfortable with the fact that we are now his pack. The internet proved to be a treasure trove of solutions.

But at the same time, it is always important to research all of the opinions because some of them out there are not the right ones. And fortunately, I had a friend who was dating a vet, and so I called them just to confirm that, you know, that was the right thing to do. And they said, "Try it. If it works, it works." And it hit.

V: Like almost all adult dogs in the rescue world, Redmond was mistreated and neglected. How has he grown since you first adopted him?

D: When the foster family first found Redmond, they were in a park at an adoption fair. There was, essentially, an outdoor pen for all of the dogs that were up for adoption. At one point they looked in the pen and someone had placed Redmond in it with the other dogs and left.

They didn't know what kind of dog he was. They didn't know what breed he was. They didn't know what his fur color was until they got him home, because his fur was so matted and filthy that he just looked like a dark-brown color. Then they gave him a bath and realized he had this really beautiful red coat, but he was also bleeding a lot because he was infested with fleas. He was in rough shape.

Part of the process of adopting a dog is understanding that you have to allow them some space to grow and to learn. At the time, he was not very good with men and a lot of it was just training him out of his impulse to get very aggressive toward older men.

I think it's really about awareness. It's about spotting your dog's triggers and training them out of it. And that comes with time, and it comes with a lot of attention to detail, because you do start to see patterns and you do start to notice what gets them scared, what gets them agitated, what gets them defensive. And that's sort of, at least for me, where I started to slowly but surely work on him in order to make him more comfortable in those situations.

And now he's pretty good with everybody, unless someone comes up from behind. That is something that I don't think I'll ever be able to get out of his system. The kind of intense, reactive surprise element of all that with him.

V: My dog Echo also gets extremely startled when people come up behind him. He is terrified of feet touching him. Many people believe they can't have a dog because of their busy schedule. You wore all the hats on your Emmy Award–winning series, *Schitt's Creek*. How did you balance work and caring for Redmond? Do you have any advice for people wanting a dog who fear their work schedule will make it impossible?

D: So, as someone who grew up with dogs, I knew that the choice to get a dog was not one that I should take lightly, because dogs do need a lot of time and a lot of attention and a lot of care. That, I think, is one of the more dangerous things about getting a dog for someone as a birthday gift or a surprise Christmas present, because you don't know whether the person you're gifting the dog to has the space in their life to really devote the time to the animal.

When I decided to get Redmond, I had the financial means to cover his vet bills. I had the resources to make sure he was taken care of even when I was working. I would not have gotten a dog if I didn't feel like I had the time, the resources, or the finances to do it. And I think that's a really important takeaway for anybody who's looking to get a dog, because so many dogs are given back, so many dogs are neglected because people underestimated just how much time and money are required in taking care of a dog and rehabilitating a dog, particularly if you're dealing with a rescue.

A lot of rescue dogs come with medical conditions, ailments that require pretty hefty bills. So, it is certainly not a choice that should be made lightly or without a lot of thought.

V: How has Redmond changed your life?

D: Redmond has changed my life in so many ways, aside from just being the most incredible companion over the past nine years. I think dogs teach you things about yourself that you might not even know. I mean, I think Redmond has taught me so much about compassion and patience and responsibility and love. That is a pretty wonderful thing, especially when you are frustrated at work, when you're tired, when you're angry.

He has just been this unbelievable mood stabilizer. And any time, you know, I'm not feeling great about myself or other people, I kind of look to him as a beacon of goodness and generosity that I hope to achieve one day. I don't think I'll get there. Nobody is quite as sweet or as levelheaded as Redmond Levy. But we can certainly strive for it.

Redmond and Dan Levy

Thirteen

RESCUE, NOT RETAIL

🐾

IT'S WORTH
THE WAIT

Rescuing a dog isn't easy.

Unlike purchasing a dog from a breeder and sending in a check, an adopter must research rescues and often submit several adoption applications before finding the perfect match. Though many people want to adopt in theory, they don't always make it to the finish line due to these obstacles. Whether they struggle to find the perfect-size puppy or a specific hypoallergenic breed, it can be a frustrating experience. But I assure you the search and red tape to rescue are worth the wait.

My aunt, uncle, and three little cousins—Max, Julian, and Lucian—got their first dog five years ago. My aunt Kay is from Korea, where only about a quarter of the population own dogs. Kay never had an interest in getting a dog until she moved to America and had kids. Then, like my parents, she didn't want to deprive her children of an important element of childhood. Plus, I'm their niece, and I always pushed for them to adopt a dog, anyway.

My cousin Max has autism, so it was important to my aunt and uncle to find a breed they knew would get along with Max and tolerate his energy. They wanted a calming, intuitive dog with patience. Kay did a lot of research and found that Cavachons (bichon frise mixed with a Cavalier King Charles spaniel) have a very good reputation with autistic children, and they were nonshedding dogs, to boot. For a year I helped Kay comb through the internet daily, looking for an adoptable Cavachon. There were many times Kay was ready to give up and just buy one, but I'd always talk her off that ledge. There are millions of amazing dogs out there that need homes. To purchase a dog usually means killing another in a shelter.

One morning I got a FaceTime call from Kay that changed everything—an adoption website had notified her of a ten-month-old male Cavachon available for adoption in Missouri. She was ecstatic but also nervous. She wanted to wait until my uncle came home from work to discuss it fully. I nipped that in the bud. I said, "Kay, you've been waiting for this dog for a year. Fill out the application *now*, because that dog isn't going to be available for long!"

Thank goodness she listened. By that same evening, their family had been approved over the phone. They were officially dog owners!

Since Kay and her family live in Maryland and the Cavachon was in Missouri, they paid a reputable transport service recommended by the rescue organization to fly him up. There was no way I was going to miss this monumental moment in my cousins' lives, so I got on the first plane to Maryland to be there when their new puppy arrived. Five years later, Mr. Kite (named after The Beatles song) is an integral part of the family. I'll let my little cousin Julian tell you all about him:

MR. KITE: THE DOG THAT'S ALWAYS THERE, BY JULIAN VASAPOLI

At some point every day when I'm at my desk attending school Zoom meetings, my dog comes walking into my room. He's a Cavachon, a combination of a bichon frise and a Cavalier King Charles spaniel. He's about the size of a laundry basket and has fluffy white fur with patches of peach, too. Mr. Kite interrupts me and comes straight through my bedroom door. He walks over and paces around my desk, his hippie necklace beads dangling from his neck, checking to see if I'm okay and probably using it as an excuse to eat some crumbs on the floor from yesterday's breakfast. Besides being interrupted sometimes, it's pretty nice to have him by my side.

Grenades?!

Before my family and I adopted our dog, he was a puppy living all the way in Missouri. I believe he was always locked in his kennel and never let out. He'd scramble for any traces of food, starving. When we adopted him, he was a ten-month-old dog; he flew on an airplane for roughly three hours to get to where we lived. By the time he arrived, he wouldn't go near any of us, except my mother. He was a bundle of fear. We named him Mr. Kite, after the song by the Beatles, "Being for the Benefit of Mr. Kite." As he grew older, his fears stayed with him. For instance, every day the mailman arrives and slides mail through the slot on our front door. Mr. Kite, being very shy and scared around strangers, barks endlessly as paper and packages come out of the metallic slot. After everything is out, Mr. Kite cautiously sniffs the pieces of paper lying on the ground, as if there were grenades or bombs in some of them.

Even now at the age of five, Mr. Kite is still a shy and scared dog.

Funny thing, though, even at times when he's sheepy, he is extremely loyal. In times of need, he's always there to comfort us. For example, when I'm having trouble with schoolwork, I can get pretty stressed and confused. When I walk over to him, he's there for me, always.

Having a dog can be a burden for some. The job of caring for Mr. Kite has taught me and my younger brother, Lucian, some responsibility. Almost every day, we have to walk Mr. Kite around the neighborhood. If he poops, I have to pick it up with my bag and carry it along until I get back home (which isn't enjoyable at all). No matter what, through snow, rain, or mud, we have to take him out. It takes

up some of my time normally reserved for schoolwork and leisure activity. Really, though, it ends up being a pretty simple and easy task.

Over the years with Mr. Kite in our lives, my family and I have come to realize that we love him more and more each day. When my little brother and I were younger, we didn't care much about Mr. Kite. We were oblivious to the fact that he was even there. He was basically invisible. Now I love him more than ever and can't bear to let him go. Even our neighbors like to have Mr. Kite around. When my neighborhood friends and I would come off the bus, my mother would be holding Mr. Kite on a leash as she walked to the bus stop. Many of my friends would swarm around him. They'd pet and give him belly rubs. Some of them said they wanted a dog, too. One time, I even went on Petfinder with them to find dogs they could adopt.

I know for a fact that my family and I couldn't imagine what we would do without Mr. Kite in our lives. Without him, we are incomplete. Dogs warm us inside with their loyalty, kindness, and love. Even if they chase chipmunks up trees, bark every time the mailman comes, and scour for crumbs on the floor, it's all worth it.

— *Julian Varagoli*

Julian, Lucian, and Mr. Kite

Tips for Crate Training Your Puppy

I know crate training can seem cruel to those unfamiliar with the practice, and you might want to give in at 3 a.m. when your puppy is wailing away, but be strong! Crate training has many benefits, including making potty training easier, kicking separation anxiety early, and keeping your dog safe from chewing on items in your home and swallowing harmful things. It also makes traveling with your dog a breeze!

When getting a puppy that's coming from being with its litter and/or mom, it's important to remember that this is the first time the puppy will be sleeping on its own. Purchasing a PLUSH TOY WITH A HEARTBEAT FEATURE can be very comforting to a little puppy. The heartbeat sound and feeling mimic sleeping in a pile of its siblings or curled up next to Mama. Warning: If your puppy likes to completely destroy toys, this might not be the right option for you as parts of this toy can be harmful if ingested.

BULLY STICKS are a game changer! Although these are the most expensive bone alternatives, they're the safest and will last your pup a long time. As someone who is always searching for deals, I buy my bully sticks at Costco. (Costco, please sponsor me. The is the second time I'm recommending one of your products.) They come in a twelve pack for around thirty bucks. If you really want to stretch your dollars, use a saw to cut the twelve-inch bully sticks into three- or four-inch pieces. You'll have a plethora of bully sticks that'll keep your teething puppy gnawing for hours!

PUT THE CRATE BY YOUR BEDSIDE. Sleeping by your puppy can be very helpful in crate training. For one, if your puppy sees you're sleeping, it might follow your lead and sleep, too. It also makes for quick trips outside when your puppy whines to go out. A tip I learned from Amelie at Mutt Scouts: if your puppy is still crying by your bedside, consider elevating the crate using two chairs so your puppy can see you and feel safe.

When bringing your puppy out to use the bathroom in the middle of the night, make it a mission with a goal. LEASH OR CARRY YOUR PUPPY DIRECTLY OUTSIDE TO DO ITS BUSINESS and then immediately put it back in the crate. It's important to teach your puppy that nighttime is for sleeping and not for playing.

PUT A SHEET OR TOWEL OVER YOUR PUPPY'S CRATE.
Dogs instinctively love caves. By making the crate cave-like and cozy, your puppy will want to go in there to feel safe.

PUT A DURABLE BLANKET OR TOWEL INSIDE THE CRATE AND HIDE KIBBLE AND TREATS IN BETWEEN THE FOLDS. This will keep your puppy occupied and make them associate the crate with treats.

NEVER FORCE YOUR PUPPY INTO HIS OR HER CRATE. Use treats and positive reinforcement to lure him or her into the crate on their own so as not to make it feel like a punishment.

TRY FEEDING YOUR PUPPY INSIDE ITS CRATE, especially if you have other dogs. Again, it's another way to make them associate the crate with positive things!

CASEY AND CANYON STANTON

"There's no way." I turned to Victoria, one hand petting Echo while the other scrolled through my phone. Unlike Victoria, I always lived in a household with dogs. My family had seven of them growing up, a mix of dogs we adopted, dogs from breeders, and admittedly, one from a puppy store.

"Yes, there is," Victoria replied matter-of-factly.

While living in California, I was asked to produce a play and move to Manhattan for the summer where I stayed with Vic, Echo, and Rue in their Chelsea apartment. One afternoon, Victoria decided that once I returned home, I'd need a companion in the form of a dog. I, on the other hand, wasn't so sure. I had every excuse in the book: I have too much work, there's no time, it's too expensive . . . And what about my schedule? I like to go out at night. But Victoria wasn't having any of it: "No, no, no—you'll figure it out. You're literally the perfect candidate to rescue. You don't have a normal nine-to-five. You do have time!"

If you haven't had the pleasure of meeting Victoria, let me tell you, she has a way of convincing people. The way I lovingly describe her to others is, "She can sell a pencil to a pencil salesman." Determined, yes. Will she back down when she believes in something strongly enough? Not a chance.

I was still hesitant. I thought having a pet would limit my freedom. So, I did something a bit manipulative to squash the conversation. I challenged her. I gave her an obstacle I thought would make adoption impossible. I looked Victoria in the eye and said, "If you can find me a bearded collie or sheepdog that doesn't shed and has blue eyes and speckled velvety ears like Echo"—now coined as "Echo ears"—"I'll adopt it."

There was no way she'd ever find my dream dog. My requirements were outrageous, unreasonable, and unattainable. I may have well asked for a unicorn that spoke three languages. I should've known that nothing would get in the way of Victoria's determination.

Both Victoria and I moved to LA at the end of that summer. A few weeks after our dog conversation, I woke up to a text from Victoria. She'd done it. She'd found a litter of Old English sheepdogs—three, to

be exact—owner-surrendered in El Paso, Texas. One had blue eyes, they in fact did not shed, and they all had freckles on their ears. Game over.

After getting a hold of the shelter and a few trips back and forth to T.J. Maxx (my favorite place to shop for dog supplies, thanks to Victoria) and Petco, I was at least 50 percent more ready to adopt a dog. I still had my doubts, though. I was fearful of the unknown, but I made the decision to walk in faith and do it anyway. At the start of the week, Victoria sent me a text pic of the most gorgeous Old English Sheepdog litter in El Paso, Texas, and by that weekend, we were on our way to pick up the very last puppy of the litter, my blue-eyed baby.

The night before we left for El Paso, I slept over at Victoria's. We woke up at 3 a.m., packed up her Jeep with dog supplies, Rue, Echo, and plenty of snacks (because what's a road trip without dogs and plenty of snacks?), and hit the road. Halfway through the drive, we pulled over on the side of the road to answer a FaceTime call from one of the shelter volunteers, whom I still speak with to this day. He showed me my future dog, jumping and playing in the red-hot Texas dirt with tons of other pups. I had tears in my eyes. My meter of 50 percent uncertainty dropped to around 15 percent.

Twelve hours later, we arrived in El Paso and stayed at La Quinta, a dog-friendly hotel with no pet fee that Victoria and I might as well be spokespeople for. We were exhausted from the drive and ate mediocre Mediterranean food in bed that we'd picked up from a shopping center in the middle of nowhere. I was nervous; I wanted to get a good night's rest knowing that the next day would be life changing, but it was hard to lie still.

I awoke the next morning incredibly antsy. It felt like I was going on a first date. *Will he like me? What should I wear? Is my hair okay?* Victoria was so patient through all my anxieties. She'd been through this many times and understood first-time jitters, so she helped calm me down. I'll always be grateful for her support. As we drove to the shelter, I couldn't shake off all my nerves, but then I remembered a saying: *You can be scared and that's okay. But you're going to do it anyway.*

We pulled up to the shelter, and it was unlike any we had seen in New York or LA. It was a small stationary trailer with no signage and a chain-link fence with barbed wire all around. "Do you think this is it?" I asked. I made Victoria drive around to make sure, but really, I just needed a few minutes to gather myself and work up the courage to take this leap.

I wanted to do something to thank those at the shelter, so I decided to bring everyone breakfast—two dozen different breakfast pastries and a few cases of canned puppy food. As I walked in, precariously balancing the pastry boxes and the cans, everything went silent. We got a ton of weird looks from people in the waiting area as we approached an older gentleman wearing a cowboy hat behind a desk.

"Hi, I'm Casey," I said. "I think I spoke to you on the phone about a dog adoption."

The man perked up. "Oh, you're the one who drove all the way from California for Sweeney? You must really think this dog is special." I felt my uncertainty barometer rise again. I looked at Victoria, who shrugged, then gave me a look that told me we were going to be okay.

"I'll go get your dog," he said, disappearing outside. I was anxious to finally see this mystery dog in person. A woman came in with a white-and-red fluffy dog slung over her shoulder like a sack of potatoes. Compared to all the young Chihuahuas in the kennels, he was huge. "Here you go," she said.

"That's it? He's mine?"

"Yep."

He was covered in dirt and urine, and as soon as I picked him up, he pooped on me from being so nervous (I'd later learn this dog had a lot of anxiety to get over). I didn't care—I just wanted him to feel safe and unafraid. The woman had us follow her into the back so I could hose him off as well as my shoes and leggings. Victoria and I peeked through a small window over the sink and saw dozens of dirty dogs shoulder to shoulder in the backyard. We looked at each other in shock. We knew we had to get him out of there. After I signed the adoption papers, it was finally time to introduce him to Echo and Rue. I wanted them so badly to like him. He was terrified, and they knew to give him time. I sat in the back just hugging him, stroking his back, admiring his freckled ears, and burying kisses into his belly.

I called my mom crying from the car. It was emotional. It's a powerful feeling, committing to caring for another living being for the rest of its life. It's a responsibility. It's fear. It's love. My barometer of uncertainty had decreased completely. This was my baby.

I'd originally chosen Matcha as a name, but upon meeting him, Victoria bluntly declared, "He is *so* not a Matcha," and I agreed. While driving through deserts and mountains to get back to Los Angeles, I kept seeing exit signs that included the word *canyon* along the way. I tested a few names aloud—Scout, River, Brody, Bodhie— but the only thing that stuck was Canyon.

Once settled back in California, I had to figure out how to be a dog parent. He was learning to trust me, and I was learning to trust my ability to care for him. Canyon was very shy. He was terrified of men, bicycles, elevators, stairs, cell phones, loud noises, the television—pretty much anything and everything. If I hung up my phone and put it on the counter too loud, the sound of it hitting the granite would make him jump. The first year and a half was incredibly challenging. I often called Victoria crying when I felt it was too much. *It shouldn't be this hard*, I thought.

One day I came home to discover that Canyon had gone wild. The legs to my table had been gnawed, my favorite sneakers had been chewed, and his bed had been shredded—fur and feathers were everywhere. Pee was on the carpets. It was a disaster. I called Victoria crying again. After letting me get out all my frustration, Victoria took a long pause and said, "Casey . . . if you're truly unhappy, I'll help you find him a great home. Dogs are supposed to enhance your life, not inhibit it."

Casey and Canyon

I went silent and considered it. I thought hard about what my life would look like without him. I took a breath and said wholeheartedly, "No, I can't do that." I was instantly taken back to the day that we got him, sitting in the back of her Jeep with this tiny puppy wrapped up in my arms. I looked into his eyes and promised to take care of him to the best of my ability for the rest of his life. I wasn't going to break a long-term promise over a short-term inconvenience.

It's true that the first six months to a year with a new dog can be challenging. You have to be patient and remember it takes time to adjust. It's normal to feel frustrated and exhausted, but don't most great things in life start that way? Canyon has changed my life in so many ways. He's expanded my capacity not only to love but also to forgive. He has taught me the power of pause. Being his mom is a responsibility I cherish, and I quite literally would die for him.

There's comfort in having an animal around you. Even on the days when I'm buried in work with my head down at my computer, I know that Canyon is there with me. Every shoe and toy that was ruined when he was a puppy, every sleepless night crate training with him—I wouldn't change it for the world. Yes, the puppy phase is challenging, but that's just what it is—a *phase*. Soon, everything you do for them becomes second nature.

Sometimes I watch Canyon when he's outside sitting in the sunlight. He'll sniff the air with his eyes closed, chin tilted up toward the sky. Sometimes he'll lazily watch the clouds or a butterfly pass by. It's beautiful. I melt over the way he plays with butterflies, and how the herder in him kicks in when he sees a squirrel. He's brought back a childlike innocence in me; he reminds me to stop and take in the wonders around me. He's my protector, my guardian angel. If I'd listened to my fear and doubt, I would've never experienced this joy. To reiterate one piece of advice to new dog and puppy parents everywhere, *You're never really ready, but do it anyway.*

It'll be worth it.

— Carey Stanton

Fourteen

HAVE A BALL

JOINING THE DOG COMMUNITY AND EMBRACING THE CULTURE

I may have been born in proximity to fame,

but dog rescue and adoption have been the things that have provided me with more purpose and passion than I'll ever truly be able explain, especially in a book! I always say I don't trust people who don't like dogs, and that still rings so true. Dogs attract some of the best people, whether they're the kind neighbors I bump into while walking my dogs, the Mutt Scouts team who've become true friends, the sweet families who adopted my fosters, or even the nice strangers I meet at the dog park who brighten my day with great conversation. Being a dog owner has given me a community that makes life more worth living. Not to mention that having the adorable, constant charm of an unwavering furry companion isn't too bad, either.

Obviously, I'm not the only one whose life has been changed for the better by a pup. As I hope you've gleaned from the many contributor stories in this book, dogs are changing lives left and right!

HAPPY AND TONY BENNETT

My dog Happy might be my biggest fan, as when I rehearse at my piano in my apartment, she is always on her dog pillow at my side. When I am sketching, she is always sitting on her pillow in my art studio. Her daily companionship is something I cherish each and every day, and she makes me happy. She is pure joy.

— *Tony Bennett*

I mean, Tony Bennett's and my stories being printed side by side is life changing on its own. But to have a one-of-a-kind sketch by Tony Bennett himself of his beloved dog Happy made *especially* for my book? I would never have thought it possible. But once again, dogs made it happen. How magical is that?

Just like Happy is always beside Tony, my dogs, Rue, Echo, and Alfie, are always by my side, but I'm *their* biggest fan. They've inspired me in all aspects of my life. They're responsible for my career, the source of my creativity and fun, and they're the reason I wake up every morning (no, really—at 6:30 a.m. Echo is in my face demanding his breakfast). What I've learned from the many contributor stories in this book is that, in a way, my story is not a unique one—dogs are bringing love, joy, and comfort to so many people.

For this reason, I love getting updates and photos from my foster adopters who've crossed to the other side and have been enchanted by the magic of dogs. With each update, I feel like my pup family has grown. I also, of course, love seeing these pups get the loving forever homes they deserve. Not only have my foster dogs changed my life for the better, but they've changed all these people's lives, too . . .

"We decided to adopt a puppy in the midst of the pandemic. I was always excited for the day I'd get a dog of my own, and this did not disappoint. Mochi is easygoing and loves to join us on our adventures. She is the gentlest, most cuddly dog. She is part of the family, the gentlest soul and a constant source of entertainment and laughter. Can't imagine life without her now!"

— Ashley and Dan, adopters of Mochi, f.k.a. P!nk from the Pup Stars

"There's a time in a boy's life when he needs a loyal companion. Duncan came into our lives right when we needed him most. He has taught my son responsibility, dedication, and everlasting love. I can't wait to watch these two grow up together."

—The Hafeli family, adopters of Duncan, f.k.a. Colby from the Charcuterie litter

"She brings so much joy to my life. I love giving and receiving unconditional love!"

—Cooper, age nine, big brother to Izzie, f.k.a. Apricot from the Charcuterie litter

"Ruth fills a space in our lives we always want present. A relationship centered around growth, learning, companionship, and adventure. She makes our lives more whole."

—Connor and Julie, adopters of Ruth, f.k.a. Apple from the Charcuterie litter

"We are so thankful to Victoria and Mutt Scouts for rescuing our dog Chessy. Because she spent the first few weeks of her life with such a great foster, she is a fearless and spunky puppy with so much love to give. She has changed our lives for the better and we cannot imagine living without her!"

—Kendall and Amanda, adopters of Chessy, f.k.a. Primrose of the Flower Children

"I was so nervous to make the leap into being a pet owner—sort of ridiculously nervous. I'm so happy Victoria convinced me to take a leap and adopt my little dog, Dot! From making me laugh every single day, taking my mind off of work, and getting me outside every day for a lovely walk, Dot's really changed my life in the best way possible, and I'm so glad I have my little sidekick."

—Daisy, adopter of Dot, f.k.a. Dahlia of the Flower Children

"My girlfriend and I adopted Jodie as a puppy in the middle of a pandemic. We were unsure if this was the best decision ever or the worst. With incredible support and guidance from Victoria it didn't take long until we decided we absolutely needed Jodie in our lives. She has turned our world upside down in the best possible way and has already taught me so many life lessons in such a short amount of time. She's made every day a happier one, and I am madly in love!"

—Tara, adopter of Jodie, f.k.a. Petunia of the Flower Children

"We're very grateful to have Roscoe in our lives! He has shown us unconditional love while also teaching us the importance of patience and trust. Roscoe reminds us to be present and to always stop and smell (or eat) the flowers!"

—Ryan and Lucas, adopters of Roscoe, f.k.a. Shawn Mendes of the Pup Stars

"Rescuing has changed our lives forever in the best way. Hazel chose us the minute we looked at her, and she has made our family more full of love, laughter, and so many cuddles. We're so proud being her parents."

—Sarah and Jason, adopters of Hazel, f.k.a. Magnolia of the Flower Children

"We feel so lucky to have our little street mutt, Cash, in our lives. He's a BIG personality in a tiny body and is spunky and sassy and makes us laugh every day. To try and sum up how our lives have been impacted since adopting him is nearly impossible because I hardly remember what life was like before him. He has made our home feel complete, and his four-legged big sister is the happiest she has ever been! We are truly grateful."

—Melanie and Greg, adopters of Cash, f.k.a. Walnut from the Charcuterie litter

"Rescue has changed my life entirely! It introduced me to a community of incredible people, and, most of all, it showed me how deeply I could love. From fostering to helping bring awareness to dogs who need homes via social media, to joining a rescue mission and adopting not one but two rescue pups—Paisley and Buey—the journey has been life changing every step of the way.

Our rescue pups have shaped who we are as humans. They have taught us the meaning of unconditional love and how to live each day to the fullest. We are grateful for every moment spent with our rescue dogs and we know that they are too. It might sound cliché, but I truly feel like the one who was rescued. My husband and I are forever grateful for the rescues Mutt Scouts and Heavenly Angels Animal Rescue who led us to our 'fur children.'"

—Morgan, adopter of Buey, f.k.a. Fig of the Charcuterie litter

"My wife introduced me to the world of rescue, and I will be forever grateful for that. It's changed my life because it has evolved my understanding of love through a relationship built on an unspoken trust. It's truly the most special bond between a human and a rescue pup. Our rescues Paisley and Buey have taught us that it doesn't matter where we come from or what our backgrounds are. All that matters are the unconditional love and mutual respect for one another. It creates such a beautiful dependency that cannot be matched. We are so grateful for **Mutt Scouts and Heavenly Angels Animal Rescue** that led us to both **Paisley and Buey.**"

—Pete, adopter of Buey, f.k.a. Fig from the Charcuterie litter

"We love Fisher so much. Rescuing him made us able to expand our pack. He has given our older rescue girl Roxy a playmate and has been a ray of sunshine in these unique days. He makes our family complete. Thank you to all rescue organizations for all you do!"

—The Moxley-Stockton family, adopters of Fisher, f.k.a. Harry Styles of the Pup Stars

HAVE A BALL

"When Charles and I moved to California from Chicago, we knew we wanted to expand our family and adopt a dog. We waited until we got out to the West Coast because the idea of walking a dog in a blizzard didn't really seem fair to anyone. We got a place in a dog-friendly apartment and started our search, all the while knowing we wanted a puppy, and we wanted a rescue. Adopting a dog in LA is about as competitive as finding a parking space, and it took us about a year and a half for the stars to align. We got our perfect boy, Bingo, on July 1, 2020. Having a dog highlights all of the joys of being alive: caring for others, falling in love, making mistakes and learning to correct them, and seeing the world through another person's (or, in this case, puppy's) eyes. It's challenging, hilarious, sweet, and fun, and it has totally changed us for the better. We can't imagine our lives without Bingo, especially because we had kind of run out of things to talk about at that point during the COVID-19 quarantine, and also because he brings so much happiness to us and everyone he meets. When you rescue, you are getting such a special dog—there's no one else like Bingo in the world! It's something that makes our life with him even more precious. How lucky are we to care for this one-in-a-million mutt?"

—Julie, adopter of Bingo, f.k.a. Oak of the Flower Children

There's really no grandiose concluding speech I can offer—I could fill this book with tons of heartwarming stories about adoption and rescue, but at the end of the day, there's still a lot of work to be done. As I hope you've learned from the stories in this book, fostering and adopting a dog are weighty yet fulfilling commitments. Caring for these animals takes time, patience, and serious dedication—but the reward is so, so worth it. When it comes to fostering, you not only save a dog's life, but you change the lives of that dog's

new family. Not to mention there's no way you come out of a foster experience the same as when you went into it, so *you* change for the better, too. When it comes to adopting, it isn't very different: you save a dog's life, and in return, your new furry family member changes *your* life. If this book has sparked your curiosity or tugged at your heartstrings, contact your local rescue and ask about ways you can help. Open your heart and your home to a pup in need. Become an ally to these great organizations and join your local dog community. I promise we've got some of the kindest, silliest, most passionate people, and you'll have a ball with us. So, let me be the first to formally welcome you to the best community, the best culture: pup culture.

P.S. In April 2021, I adopted a little boy puppy. I named him Callaway—"Cal" for short—after my dear friend Emily Callaway.

ACKNOWLEDGMENTS

There are so many people I want to thank for helping and supporting me in the making of this book. The obvious first being my family—Mom and Dad, thank you for caving in and adopting my first dog. To my brother, Will: thank you for being my biggest cheerleader. You're never surprised to hear how many dogs I have at the house, and you'll always say, "Aw," to every single one of them. Thank you to Aunt Kay, Uncle Dennis, and my little cousins for humoring my doggy dreams. Without my family's constant support and encouragement, this book would have been thrown out several meltdowns ago.

To my amazing contributors—David Letterman, Glenn Close, Vanessa Williams, Dan Levy, and Tony Bennett—I'm still pinching myself that you were willing to share your dog stories with me. Thank you to Julian, the brightest eleven-year-old I know and a rescue advocate in the making, and thank you as well to my dear friends Casey and Maysie, and to the Mutt Scouts community of adopters and volunteers who told their stories and trusted me enough to adopt my precious puppies. To Nikki Audet and Dr. Gary Weitzman, thank you for sharing your experiences and expertise to help others.

To Dub Cornett: you gave me my first producer job and told me I could write a book when I thought I couldn't. You wear many hats to me—boss, manager, mentor, fellow dog lover, and, of course, great friend. I'm so glad Echo barked through our very first phone call.

To my supportive friends Andria, Casey, Courtney, Gabby, Greg, Lauren, Maysie, Rachel, and, of course, Zoe. I put your names in alphabetical order as to not show favoritism (haha). You guys know how much I appreciate you, so I won't get all mushy. Thank you for lifting me up when I needed it most throughout the entire process of writing this book.

To the Mutt Scouts: wow. You've changed my life. I'm so honored to be a part of the team. I never had any interest in being a Girl Scout in grade school, but I sure am thrilled to be a Mutt Scout. I've finally met a group of strong women who love and care for dogs as much as I do! There's so much work left to do, but there's no doubt in my mind that we can do it.

To my editorial team who put up with me—Natasha Yglesias, Anja Schmidt, Sam Ford, and the rest at Tiller Press at Simon & Schuster—thank you. I'm so appreciative of your hard work, patience, and edits. Thank you for making this happen and for helping me not sound like an idiot!

And last but certainly not least, to Rue, Echo, and Alfie: "Woof!" No, I'm kidding. I love you three. Thank you for being the best foster siblings. Thank you for inspiring me. Thank you for being my 24/7 support system, for being my protectors and companions, and for your unconditional love. We humans don't deserve dogs.

ABOUT THE AUTHOR

Victoria Lily Shaffer is no stranger to showbiz, having practically grown up on the set of the *Late Show with David Letterman*. She's the vice president of creative development at Oso Studios where she most notably produced the series *Extra Innings with Bill Murray & Brian Doyle-Murray* for Facebook Watch. Shaffer was the host of Pet Life Radio's *Tails of the City*, which streamed on iHeartRadio, and she's also worked on productions such as the annual Tony and Emmy awards, *Jimmy Kimmel Live!*, HBO's *Divorce*, and Netflix's *My Next Guest Needs No Introduction with David Letterman*. Victoria has combined her love for showbiz with her passion for animal rescue advocacy, creating content to inspire others to #adoptdontshop. She's the head of outreach and puppy guru at Mutt Scouts, a rescue based in San Diego and Los Angeles, and dreams of starting her own leash and collar line one day. Follow Victoria on Instagram (@victorialilyshaffer) to meet her latest fosters (usually large numbers of adorable newborn puppies). This is her debut publication.